INSTRUCTOR'S EDITION

Microsoft® Visio®
2016: Part 1

 **Read Me First!**

Congratulations on selecting CHOICE courseware! This quick guide will give you access to key instructor resources so you can present the best possible CHOICE learning experience.

The CHOICE Instructor's Edition

This Instructor's Edition is a crucial tool that provides you with all the course-specific technical and setup information, delivery notes, and instructional material that you need as a training professional to deliver an excellent learning experience to your students.

The CHOICE Facilitator's Guide

Before presenting this or any CHOICE course, make sure you explore the CHOICE Facilitator's Guide for critical information about virtual and blended course delivery techniques and the CHOICE instructional philosophy and learning experience. Get access to the CHOICE Facilitator's Guide through the CHOICE Facilitator's Course.

The CHOICE Facilitator's Course

You can find the CHOICE Facilitator's Guide and other great resources for delivering Logical Operations courseware products through the free CHOICE Facilitator's Course. To access the free Facilitator's Course, simply:

1. Visit www.lo-choice.com
2. Enter access key **LCSYB24YEF**
3. Download and explore the CHOICE Facilitator's Guide!

The Logical Operations Instructor Community

Logical Operations leads a very active online community and resource center where instructors from all over the world share their ideas, interact, and engage with each other. Join the community from the CHOICE Facilitator's Course, or search www.linkedin.com for the "Logical Operations Instructor Community" group to join the conversation. Again, congratulations on your choice—the right choice—the Logical CHOICE!

Microsoft® Visio®
2016: Part 1

Microsoft® Visio® 2016: Part 1

Part Number: 091071
Course Edition: 1.0

Acknowledgements

PROJECT TEAM

Author	Production Support	Media Designer	Content Editor
Nagaraj D R	Tamara Hagen	Brian Sullivan	Catherine M. Albano

Notices

Microsoft® Visio® 2016: Part 1

Using the Microsoft® Visio® 2016: Part 1 Instructor's Edition

Welcome to the Instructor

Welcome and congratulations on your choice to use the finest materials available on the market today for expert-facilitated learning in any presentation modality. You can utilize the *Microsoft® Visio® 2016: Part 1* curriculum to present world-class instructional experiences whether:

- Your students are participating with you in the classroom or virtually.
- You are presenting in a continuous event or in an extended teaching plan, such as an academic semester.
- Your presentation takes place synchronously with the students or asynchronously.
- Your students have physical courseware or are using digital materials.
- You have any combination of these instructional dimensions.

To make the best use of the *Microsoft® Visio® 2016: Part 1* materials in any or all of these dimensions, be sure to review the contents of the CHOICE Facilitator's Guide for an orientation to all of the components of the CHOICE experience.

Preparing to Present the CHOICE Experience

Effectively presenting the information and skills in this course requires adequate preparation in any presentation modality. As such, as an instructor, you should familiarize yourself with the content of the entire course, including its organization and instructional approaches. You should review each of the student activities, exercises, and Mastery Builders so you can facilitate them during the learning event. Also, make sure you review the tips for presenting in the different dimensions; these instructor tips are available as notes in the margins of your Instructor's Edition.

In addition to the curriculum itself, Microsoft® PowerPoint® slides, data files, and other course-specific support material may be available by downloading the files from the CHOICE Course screen. Be sure to obtain the course files prior to your learning event and make sure you distribute them to your students.

Course Facilitator Icons

Throughout the Instructor's Edition, you may see various instructor-focused icons that provide suggestions, answers to problems, and supplemental information for you, the instructor.

Icon	Description
	A **display slide** note provides a prompt to the instructor to display a specific slide from the provided PowerPoint files.
	Content delivery tips provide guidance for specific delivery techniques you may want to utilize at particular points in the course, such as lectures, whiteboard sketching, or performing your own demonstrations for the class.
	Managing learning interactions provide suggested places to interact with the class as a whole. You might poll the class with closed-ended questions, check comprehension with open-ended questions, conduct planned discussion activities, or take notes and questions from the group to "park" and address at a later point in the class.
	Monitoring learner progress notes suggest when you might want to monitor individual students as they perform activities, or have private sidebar conversations with specific individual participants.
	Engaging learners notes suggest opportunities to involve the students in active ways with the course presentation, such as enabling them to demonstrate their work to the class as a whole, or checking in on the logistics of the presentation.
	Incorporating other assets notes suggest when and how to include other types of media, such as visiting CHOICE social media sites, accessing specific web resources, or utilizing media assets provided with the course, such as Logical Operations' LearnTOs.
	Additional notes show where, on occasion, there may be instructor notes or tips that appear in a separate section at the back of the courseware and not in the margins.

Digital Software Updates

The software vendor may at any time deploy software updates digitally, resulting in changes that may not be reflected dynamically in this course. Stay up to date with product updates and be ready to adapt the material to any changes in the user interface.

Presentation Tips for the Microsoft® Visio® 2016: Part 1 Course

Here are some useful tips for presenting the *Microsoft® Visio® 2016: Part 1* course.

Although this course was developed using Microsoft® Windows® 10 as the operating system, it should be possible to present the course using Windows 8, Windows 7, or other earlier versions of Windows with only minor keying variations. However, Logical Operations did not keycheck the course in other environments and does not guarantee specific outcomes if you alter the setup.

For training organizations that choose to utilize the Windows® 8, Windows® 7, Windows Vista®, or Windows® XP operating system within class, please note that course activity instructions may need to be amended slightly by the instructor during class to ensure students (particularly those who have only basic PC knowledge) are able to navigate through course activities.

In general, for prior operating system versions, instructors should tell students to open and access any Microsoft® Office Professional Edition 2016 software through the Windows **Start** button or a desktop icon. After accessing the software, students and instructors should be able to follow the activity instructions with only minimal potential discrepancies.

Course–Specific Technical Requirements

Hardware

For this course, you will need one computer for each student and one for the instructor. Each computer will need the following minimum hardware configurations:

- 1 GHz or faster 32-bit (x86) or 64-bit (x64) processor with SSE2 instruction set
- 1 gigabyte (GB) RAM (32-bit) or 2 GB RAM (64-bit)
- 3 GB of available hard disk space
- Keyboard and mouse (or other pointing device)
- Graphics hardware acceleration requires DirectX 10 graphics card (1,280 × 800 resolution monitor recommended)
- DVD-ROM drive (if installing any software from a DVD-ROM)
- Network cards and cabling for local network access
- Internet access with no password required (through Wi-Fi, cabled Ethernet, or mobile broadband)
- Printer (optional) or an installed printer driver
- Projection system to display the instructor's computer screen

Software

- Microsoft® Windows® 10
- Microsoft® Visio® Professional 2016
- Microsoft® Office Professional 2010 or higher

Setting Up the Course

For each student and the instructor:

- Provide a system with Internet access and the given hardware requirements.
- Install Microsoft Windows 10.
- Install Microsoft Visio Professional 2016.
- Install Microsoft Office Professional 2010 or higher.

File Extensions

For each student and the instructor computer:

1. On the Windows 10 desktop, on the taskbar, select **File Explorer**.
2. Select the **View** tab.
3. In the **Show/hide** group, check the **File name extensions** check box.
4. Close the File Explorer window.

Prior to Each Class

Prior to each running of the class, the instructor should:

1. Create a folder named **091071Data** on the C drive of the instructor's computer and on each learner's computer.
2. Copy the course data files from the CD-ROM into the **091071Data** folder. If the instructor has already run the course in the same classroom, he or she should first delete all of the data files in the **091071Data** folder and then copy fresh versions of the data files into that folder. This will ensure every running of the class uses fresh data files.

Install the Course Data Files

From the course **Files** tile on CHOICE, download and extract the **091071CD<version>.zip** file. From the location you extracted the files to, navigate to the **091071CD<version>**

\091_071\091071Data folder. Run the **091071Data.exe** file, which will install a folder named **091071Data** at the root of your C drive. (You may need to select **More Info** and then select **Run Anyway** if prompted by Windows.) This folder contains all the lesson-specific subfolders and data files you will need to run this course. There is a separate folder with the starter files for each lesson or Mastery Builder, and there may be a Solutions folder with completed files students can use to check their results.

Presentation Planners

The lesson durations given in the course content are estimates based on a typical class experience. The following planners show examples of how the content could be presented in either a continuous one-day flow or separately across a multi-session seminar series. Your presentation flow may vary based on a number of factors, including the size of the class, whether students are in specialized job roles, whether you plan to incorporate LearnTOs or other assets from the CHOICE Course screen into the course, and so on. Use the samples and blank planners to determine how you will conduct the class to meet the needs of your own situation.

Continuous Presentation: Model Class Flow

This planner provides a sample presentation flow based on approximately one 7.5-hour day of training with breaks and lunch factored in.

Section	Duration	Day Planner
Welcome and Introductions	0:30	8:30 – 9:00
Lesson 1: Getting Started with Visio 2016	1:00	9:00 – 10:00
BREAK	0:15	10:00 – 10:15
Lesson 2: Working with Workflow Diagram Tools	1:00	10:15 – 11:15
Lesson 3: Building Organization Charts	1:15	11:15 – 12:30
LUNCH	0:30	12:30 – 1:00
Lesson 4: Designing a Floor Plan	0:40	1:00 – 1:40
Lesson 5: Building a Cross-Functional Flowchart	1:00	1:40 – 2:40
BREAK	0:15	2:40 – 2:55
Lesson 6: Designing a Network Diagram	0:45	2:55 – 3:40
Lesson 7: Styling a Diagram	0:30	3:40 – 4:10

Continuous Presentation: Your Class Flow

Use this planner to plan the flow of your own training day based on the needs of your students, the schedule for your own day, and/or any other modifications you choose.

Section	Duration	Day Planner
Welcome and Introductions		
Lesson 1: Getting Started with Visio 2016		
Lesson 2: Working with Workflow Diagram Tools		
Lesson 3: Building Organization Charts		
Lesson 4: Designing a Floor Plan		
Lesson 5: Building a Cross-Functional Flowchart		
Lesson 6: Designing a Network Diagram		
Lesson 7: Styling a Diagram		

Non-continuous Presentation: Model Class Flow

This planner provides a sample presentation flow based on separate sessions presented over multiple days or weeks.

Session Number	Material Covered	Session Duration
One	Welcome and Introductions Lesson 1: Getting Started with Visio 2016 Lesson 2: Working with Workflow Diagram Tools	2:30
Two	Lesson 3: Building Organization Charts Lesson 4: Designing a Floor Plan	1:55
Three	Lesson 5: Building a Cross-Functional Flowchart Lesson 6: Designing a Network Diagram Lesson 7: Styling a Diagram Wrap-Up and Review	2:30

Non-continuous Presentation: Your Class Flow

Use this planner to plan how you will present the course content based on the needs of your students, your conventions for the number and length of sessions, and any other modifications you choose.

Session Number	Material Covered	Session Duration

About This Course

From the earliest eras of human existence, visual images have been used to represent knowledge, data, and information. Beginning with the Paleolithic cave paintings and continuing to today's most complex computer networks, these images leverage the ability of the human brain to rapidly perceive patterns and trends from visual representations.

In today's workplace, visual diagrams are an essential part of communication, from road maps to sales flows to process charts. Microsoft® Visio® provides you with an intuitive, customizable tool to easily create a professional-looking visual product by using its extensive gallery of shapes. By following the exercises in this course, you will create visually engaging diagrams, maps, and drawings, using graphical elements to make information easier to comprehend.

Course Description

Target Student

This course is designed for persons who are new to Visio and who will be using Visio to create basic workflows and perform end-to-end flowcharting.

Course Prerequisites

To ensure your success, you will need to be familiar with using personal computers, including a mouse and keyboard. You should be comfortable in the Windows 8 environment and proficient in using Windows to access programs, navigate to information stored on the computer, and manage files and folders.

To meet this prerequisite, you can take any one or more of the following Logical Operations courses:

- *Using Microsoft® Windows® 10*
- *Microsoft® Windows® 10: Transition from Windows® 7*

Course Objectives

In this course, you will design, modify, and manage basic diagrams. You will:

- Identify the basic elements of Visio and their use.
- Create a workflow diagram.
- Build organization charts.
- Design a floor plan.
- Build a cross-functional flowchart.
- Design a network diagram.
- Style a diagram.

The CHOICE Home Screen

Logon and access information for your CHOICE environment will be provided with your class experience. The CHOICE platform is your entry point to the CHOICE learning experience, of which this course manual is only one part.

On the CHOICE Home screen, you can access the CHOICE Course screens for your specific courses. Visit the CHOICE Course screen both during and after class to make use of the world of support and instructional resources that make up the CHOICE experience.

Each CHOICE Course screen will give you access to the following resources:

- **Classroom**: A link to your training provider's classroom environment.
- **eBook**: An interactive electronic version of the printed book for your course.
- **Files**: Any course files available to download.
- **Checklists**: Step-by-step procedures and general guidelines you can use as a reference during and after class.
- **LearnTOs**: Brief animated videos that enhance and extend the classroom learning experience.
- **Assessment**: A course assessment for your self-assessment of the course content.
- Social media resources that enable you to collaborate with others in the learning community using professional communications sites such as LinkedIn or microblogging tools such as Twitter.

Depending on the nature of your course and the components chosen by your learning provider, the CHOICE Course screen may also include access to elements such as:

- LogicalLABS, a virtual technical environment for your course.
- Various partner resources related to the courseware.
- Related certifications or credentials.
- A link to your training provider's website.
- Notices from the CHOICE administrator.
- Newsletters and other communications from your learning provider.
- Mentoring services.

Visit your CHOICE Home screen often to connect, communicate, and extend your learning experience!

How to Use This Book

As You Learn

This book is divided into lessons and topics, covering a subject or a set of related subjects. In most cases, lessons are arranged in order of increasing proficiency.

The results-oriented topics include relevant and supporting information you need to master the content. Each topic has various types of activities designed to enable you to solidify your understanding of the informational material presented in the course. Information is provided for reference and reflection to facilitate understanding and practice.

Data files for various activities as well as other supporting files for the course are available by download from the CHOICE Course screen. In addition to sample data for the course exercises, the course files may contain media components to enhance your learning and additional reference materials for use both during and after the course.

Checklists of procedures and guidelines can be used during class and as after-class references when you're back on the job and need to refresh your understanding.

At the back of the book, you will find a glossary of the definitions of the terms and concepts used throughout the course. You will also find an index to assist in locating information within the instructional components of the book.

As You Review

Any method of instruction is only as effective as the time and effort you, the student, are willing to invest in it. In addition, some of the information that you learn in class may not be important to you immediately, but it may become important later. For this reason, we encourage you to spend some time reviewing the content of the course after your time in the classroom.

As a Reference

The organization and layout of this book make it an easy-to-use resource for future reference. Taking advantage of the glossary, index, and table of contents, you can use this book as a first source of definitions, background information, and summaries.

Course Icons

Watch throughout the material for the following visual cues.

Icon	Description
	A **Note** provides additional information, guidance, or hints about a topic or task.
	A **Caution** note makes you aware of places where you need to be particularly careful with your actions, settings, or decisions so that you can be sure to get the desired results of an activity or task.
	LearnTO notes show you where an associated LearnTO is particularly relevant to the content. Access LearnTOs from your CHOICE Course screen.
	Checklists provide job aids you can use after class as a reference to perform skills back on the job. Access checklists from your CHOICE Course screen.
	Social notes remind you to check your CHOICE Course screen for opportunities to interact with the CHOICE community using social media.

1 | Getting Started with Visio 2016

Lesson Time: 1 hour

Lesson Objectives

In this lesson, you will identify the basic elements of Visio and their use. You will:

- Perform basic tasks in the Visio environment.
- Use Backstage commands.
- Save a file.

Lesson Introduction

Suppose you've just received an assignment to plan the network for your company's new office space, or that your employer's sales team needs detailed directions to a convention center. Whatever the task, you've decided that a visual representation is the best way to convey the information. You know that Microsoft® Visio® 2016 is the ideal choice to create a professional diagram quickly and efficiently, but there's one problem: You've never used it.

As with any other new software, taking the time now to understand the interface and tools will allow you to get up to speed quickly while using the Visio application, and you'll be on your way to creating the informative and engaging diagrams you need. In this lesson, you will identify the basic elements of Visio and use some of the tools to carry out simple tasks in Visio 2016.

TOPIC A

Perform Basic Tasks in the Visio Environment

With Visio 2016, you have the power to create almost any type of diagram imaginable by using extensive collections of drawing elements and styles through a convenient interface. To make the best use of Visio's many capabilities, you first need to know how to navigate the user interface. Of course, you could always just open the program and start trying out commands, but in doing so you might miss some of the key features. By taking a guided tour of the main components now, you'll already know your way around when you start accessing the software. In this topic, you will perform basic tasks in the Visio environment.

Visio

Check with students to see if they have already used Visio 2016 applications and ask them to list the benefits of using the same.

Visio 2016 is a diagramming application with tools for creating professional-looking drawings to represent data, systems, and processes. Visio 2016 provides an extensive range of templates that can be used to create almost any type of diagram imaginable, from floor plans to project schedules, calendars, brainstorming maps, and more. Visio 2016 runs on Windows 7, Windows 8, or Windows 10, and is available in three versions: Standard, Professional, and Visio Pro for Office 365.

Vector Images vs. Bitmap Images

Visio is a tool that supports vector-based illustration. Vector images are made up of mathematically computed lines that result in sharp images. Bitmap images are made up of dots called pixels and are resolution-dependent. Visio, being a vector-based application, still supports the use of bitmap images such as photographs.

The Visio Drawing Interface

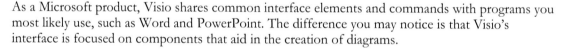

The Visio Drawing Interface

As a Microsoft product, Visio shares common interface elements and commands with programs you most likely use, such as Word and PowerPoint. The difference you may notice is that Visio's interface is focused on components that aid in the creation of diagrams.

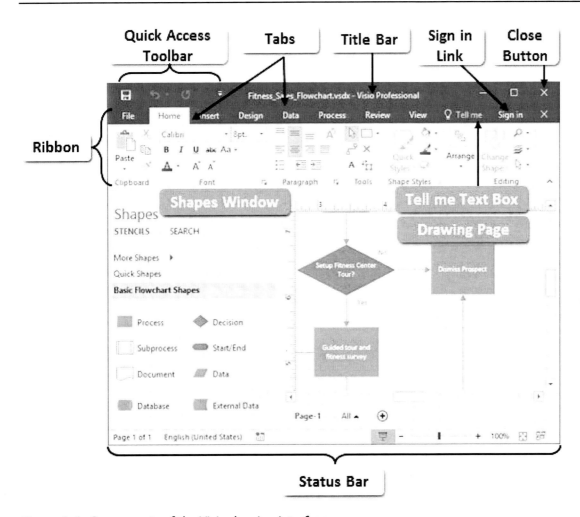

Figure 1-1: Components of the Visio drawing interface.

 Caution: The elements of the Visio drawing interface may appear differently depending on whether or not the screen is fully maximized.

The Visio drawing interface consists of two main sections, the **Shapes** window and the **Drawing** page. The functions of the various elements of the Visio drawing interface are described in the following table.

Element	Function
Title bar	Displays the name of the active document across the top of the application window. Also indicates if the program is running in any special mode.
Quick Access Toolbar	Located in the upper-left corner of the application window, this toolbar gives you rapid access to frequently used commands such as **Save**, **Undo**, and **Redo**. You can customize it to display the commands you use most frequently, and also relocate it under the ribbon.

Element	Function
Ribbon	The ribbon contains most of the commands you will use to create a drawing, organized onto labeled tabs (**Home**, **Insert**, etc.). Each tab has groups of functionally related commands, separated by a vertical dividing line with a descriptive label below the grouping. If a group contains more commands than can be displayed in the group's area, there will be a dialog box launcher 🔲 in the bottom-right corner of the group. Additional tabs may appear according to the context of your drawing's elements. For example, if you insert a picture, a **Format** tab will appear with command groups used for formatting the image.
Shapes window	A window located on the left side of the **Drawing** page that displays the shapes available for use in a drawing. Groups of shapes are organized in stencils that are stacked one over the other and can be opened or closed.
Drawing page	The drawing area occupies the central screen region, to the right of the Shapes window. Shapes can be dragged from the Shapes window onto the **Drawing** page.
Status bar	The status bar is a customizable bar located at the bottom of the application window. It holds a variety of useful controls for operations on your whole document, such as a zoom slider and macro recording button. The status bar also displays the dimensions of a selected shape on the **Drawing** page.
Close buttons	The **Close** buttons allow you to close the drawing or close the drawing window.
Sign in link	If you are signed in to **Office** when using Visio 2016, your user name and optional picture appear in the upper-right corner of the application window. Signing in makes your documents and settings available on any device you are using, even if that device doesn't have Microsoft Office.
Tell Me text box	The **Tell Me** text box allows you to search for a command or action. When you select any item from the search results, the action is performed in Visio and the resultant dialog box is displayed in the Visio interface. If the keyword that you searched for is not available, the keyword specified by you is listed below the text box, in the format "Get Help on <keyword>". This format allows you to search for the keyword in Visio 2016 online help.

Visio Ribbon Tabs

The tabs on the Visio ribbon enable you to access various Visio commands and features. Some of the tabs are contextual and appear only when you select or insert the object they control.

Visio Ribbon Tabs

Tab	Description
File	Allows you to access the **Backstage** view for whole document commands and global program settings.
Home	Contains the most frequently used commands and the command groups related to text parameters, tools, shape styles, shape arrangement, and shape modification.
Insert	Contains commands for inserting illustrations, groupings, callouts, connectors, links, and text elements.

Tab	Description
Design	Provides access to commands for defining the look of the document, such as page orientation, stylistic themes, background, and layout.
Data	Contains commands for managing external databases or spreadsheet data represented by shapes.
Process	Provides commands used in complex process diagrams.
Review	Contains commands used for proofing, language selection, and commenting.
View	Contains commands to control the screen display, including grid lines, task panes, zoom, visual aids, and macros.

ACTIVITY 1-1

Navigating the Elements of the Visio 2016 Interface

Data File

C:\091071Data\Getting Started with Visio 2016\B&B Phone Prospect Sales Process.vsdx

Before You Begin

Visio Professional 2016 has been installed on your computer. You have logged in and are ready to get started.

Scenario

The B&B Fitness Company is under new management and is reviewing its procedures. You have been assigned the task of revising sales procedures. The current sales process procedure for inbound phone prospects is represented in a Visio 2016 diagram. Because you've never used Visio, you decide that a good first step would be to open up the diagram and familiarize yourself with the Visio 2016 interface.

One of your coworkers wanted to give you a few tips and told you to make sure to turn on the grid. You are wondering what she is referring to and hope to identify the grid while getting to know the application.

> **Note:** Activities may vary slightly if the software vendor has issued digital updates. Your instructor will notify you of any changes.

Encourage the students to share their desktops and use screen-sharing annotation tools, if available, to highlight the various user interface elements. This can be utilized as an opportunity for remote learners to engage with the students in your classroom.

Notify students of any changes to activities based on digital software updates issued by the software vendor.

1. Start Visio 2016 and open the file **B&B Phone Prospect Sales Process.vsdx**.
   a) Select the **Start** button and select **All Apps**.
   b) In the list of apps, scroll down to the **V** section.
   c) Right-click **Visio 2016** and select **Pin to taskbar**.
   d) On the taskbar, select the **Visio 2016** icon.
   e) On the left side, select **Open Other Drawings**.
   f) On the right side, in the left panel, select **This PC**.
   g) On the right side, in the left panel, select **Browse**.
   h) Navigate to the **C:\091071Data\Getting Started with Visio 2016** folder.
   i) Select the file **B&B Phone Prospect Sales Process.vsdx** and select **Open** to view the contents of the file.

2. Perform basic tasks on the Visio drawing interface.
   a) Use the zoom controls in the status bar to zoom the drawing to 100 percent.

   b) From the Shapes window, drag and drop the **Document** shape `Document` to the whitespace below the flowchart on the **Drawing** page.

c) Select the recently added **Document** shape and then select the style to the left of the current style in the **Shape Styles** group.

Shape Styles

3. Modify the grid settings.

   a) Select the **View** tab and locate the **Grid** check box.

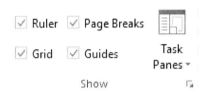

   b) Uncheck the **Grid** check box to view the drawing without a grid, and then check it again to display the grid again.
   c) In the bottom-right corner of the **Show** group, select the dialog box launcher.
   d) In the **Ruler & Grid** dialog box, in the **Grid** section, from the **Grid spacing** drop-down list for both **Horizontal** and **Vertical** grids, select **Coarse**.
   e) Select **OK**.
   f) Verify the change in the grid on the **Drawing** page and, for both the horizontal and vertical grids, repeat steps 3c and 3d, but this time select **Fine** as the grid spacing.
   g) Select the **OK** button to close the dialog box.

4. Select the newly added **Document** shape in the drawing and in the left side of the status bar, below the **Drawing** page, verify the shape's dimensions, namely width and height of the shape, are displayed in the status bar and leave the file open.

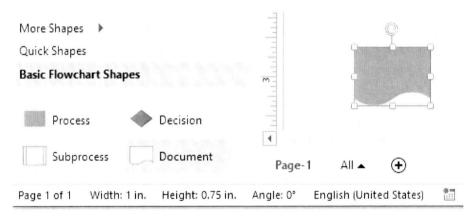

Key Drawing Components

Visio drawings are based on several primary components: templates, stencils, shapes, and connectors. Templates contain the associated stencils, page layout, and styles used to format shapes, text, and other drawing objects. The three primary types of Visio files are drawings (VSDX files), stencils (VSSX files), and templates (VSTX files).

Key Drawing Components

Templates

A *template* in Visio is a kit that contains the menus, toolbars, stencils, and shapes that you need to create a specific type of drawing, such as an organization chart or a timeline. For example, the Basic Flowchart template provides the Basic Shapes stencil, which contains six basic shapes such as start/end, diamond shape for decision, and so on.

When you create a new drawing, the first step is to select a template. You can use one of Visio's built-in templates, or you can create your own template.

Ask the students to list the benefits of creating files using templates instead of starting with a blank file.

Units of Measure

The Visio templates support two measurement units: **Metric Units** and **US Units**. When you select **Metric Units**, the page size is set to A4 and the units will be set either as millimeters or a standard metric measuring unit.

The default unit of measure is **US Units**. The measuring unit will be set either as inches or feet. The default measuring system may change according to the diagram type.

Stencils

A *stencil* is a collection of related shapes that are used to create a specific type of diagram, such as a flowchart or road map. Each stencil contains the shapes for a specific type of drawing, and you can open multiple stencils with each drawing. When a template is selected, the default stencils included in the template are automatically loaded into the Shapes window.

Shapes

Shapes

Shapes are two-dimensional entities that are the building blocks of a Visio drawing. The shapes on a Visio stencil are called the *master* shapes. Shapes are contained in stencils that are provided with the selected template. When you drag a shape from the stencil to the **Drawing** page, an instance, or copy, of the shape is placed on the page and the master remains on the stencil. Shapes have connection points to which connectors are attached.

As you create your drawing, you can also load more stencils into the Shapes window by selecting them from the **More Shapes** menu, which gives you access to stencils from every drawing category, such as Business and Engineering, no matter which template was used to create the drawing. You can also define your own custom shape.

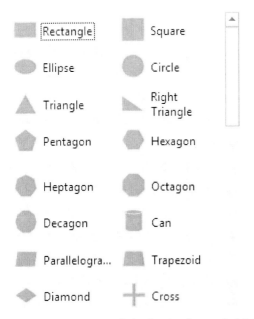

Figure 1-2: Some of the basic shapes in Visio.

Connectors

Connectors are one-dimensional entities or lines consisting of line segments that join shapes together, such as an arrow that connects one shape to the next in a flow chart. Connectors have end points that are connected to connection points on the border of a shape. Each endpoint is "glued" to a shape (either to the shape as a whole or to a specific connection point on the shape). When one of the shapes is moved, the connector stays attached and stretches as needed to maintain the connection. Connections can be created automatically as you place shapes on the drawing by using **AutoConnect**, or you can add them manually. *View Menu*

Connectors

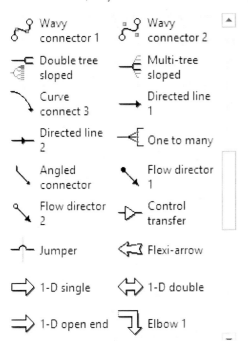

Figure 1-3: Some of the connector types in Visio.

Quick Shapes Stencil

Quick Shapes Stencil

Every stencil contains a *Quick Shapes* area at the top of it that holds four to six of the most frequently used shapes and is divided from the rest of the shapes by a thin line. When a stencil is first opened, the Quick Shapes area is populated automatically, but you can easily drag a shape in or out.

When **AutoConnect** is enabled, a mini toolbar containing the first four Quick Shapes is displayed as you draw. This can save time if your drawing contains many instances of only a few shapes, compared to dragging a shape from a stencil.

The Quick Shapes are also contained in the **Quick Shapes** stencil, which appears in the menu under **My Shapes**. When more than one stencil is open, the **Quick Shapes** area becomes a collection of the Quick Shapes from each of the stencils, separated by the names of the stencils they belong to. If you are using only a few shapes from multiple stencils, you can save time by loading each stencil's Quick Shapes with the ones you need. Then after activating the **Quick Shapes** stencil, you can drag your shapes directly from there, rather than having to switch between stencils.

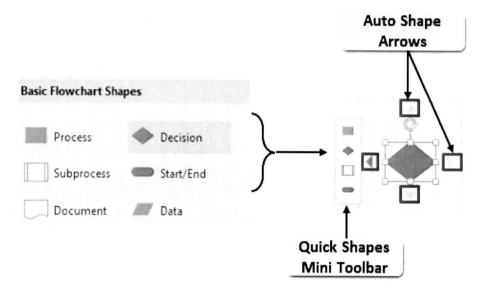

Figure 1–4: Quick Shapes stencil displayed on the left side of the shape.

The Tools Group

The Tools Group

The **Tools** group on the **Home** tab contains tools to select shapes, connectors, and text, which can often be overlapped on a drawing. It is common to switch back and forth between these tools as you create your drawing. Each of the tools has a special cursor symbol that appears when it is activated.

* **Pointer** tool: Allows you to select, move, and resize shapes and modify connections. This tool is selected automatically when a new file is opened.
* **Connector** tool: Allows you to create connections manually.
* **Text** tool: Allows you to add a text shape or select existing text.

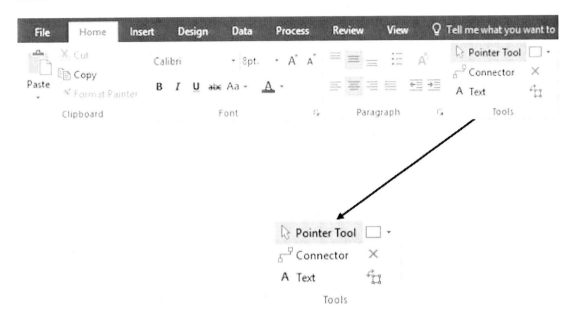

Figure 1-5: The tools available in the Tools group.

ACTIVITY 1-2
Working with Visio Drawing Elements

Data File

C:\091071Data\Getting Started with Visio 2016\B&B Phone Prospect Sales Process.vsdx

Before You Begin

The B&B Phone Prospect Sales Process.vsdx file is open.

Scenario

Now that you know more about the elements of a Visio drawing, you decide to take a closer look at the sales process diagram to identify those elements.

1. Select the tools in the **Tools** group and use **AutoConnect** to preview the connection to shapes.
    a) Select the **Home** tab in the ribbon.
    b) Select **Tools→Connector**.

    Verify that the mouse pointer changes to a plus sign with line and arrow.
    c) Select **Tools→Pointer Tool**.
    d) Select the **View** tab.
    e) Check the **AutoConnect** check box. Verify that the **Dynamic Grid** and **Connection Points** check boxes are checked.
    f) Select the **Home** tab.
    g) Move the pointer over the diamond shape in the drawing that is labeled **Setup Fitness Center Tour?** until you see four blue triangles surrounding the shape.

> **Note:** These triangles are **AutoConnect** arrows that are used when placing adjacent shapes on a drawing.

    h) Slowly move the pointer over the left **AutoConnect** arrow.

    Verify that the **Quick Shapes** mini toolbar is displayed and view the shapes in it.

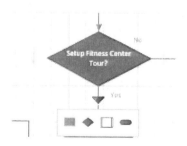

Tell students that the **Quick Shapes** mini toolbar may appear in a different place for them.

2. Change the shapes that appear in the **Quick Shapes** mini toolbar. *Be on this stencil to move Doesn't work*

   a) In the **Quick Shapes** area of the **Basic Flowchart Shapes** stencil, select the **Document** shape and drag it to where the **Start/End** shape is located in the left pane.

      Verify that the **Document** shape and the **Start/End** shape have exchanged places.

   b) Move the pointer over the diamond shape labeled **Setup Fitness Center Tour?**, verify that the **AutoConnect** arrows are displayed, and move the pointer slowly over the left arrow.

      Verify that the **Quick Shapes** mini toolbar now contains the **Document** shape instead of the **Start/End** shape.

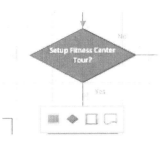

Reasons for Customizing the Interface

As you draw different types of diagrams, you may find yourself with different viewing needs. Visio allows you to customize many aspects of the interface, such as the status bar and the **Quick Access Toolbar**, according to your personal preferences. You can also import or export customizations.

 Access the Checklist tile on your CHOICE Course screen for reference information and job aids on How to Customize the Interface.

Ask the students to list some of the customizations that they would carry out in Visio along with their reasoning for doing so.

Zoom and Pan

Two of the most important operations used in viewing a document are zoom and pan. *Zoom* increases or decreases the magnification, enabling you to zoom in and zoom out of specific areas of a drawing to view things more clearly. In fact, Visio provides an automatic zoom that engages when you are adding text. *Pan* shifts the center point of the view to another part of the drawing.

Zoom and Pan

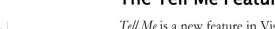

Figure 1-6: Flow chart viewed in the PAN & ZOOM window.

| | Access the Checklist tile on your CHOICE Course screen for reference information and job aids on How to Zoom and Pan. |

The Tell Me Feature

The Tell Me Feature

Tell Me is a new feature in Visio 2016 that enables you to quickly find specific functions or commands within the Visio interface. The **Tell me what you want to do** text box allows you to type the name of a function or command that you want to locate and displays updated search results every time you press a key to specify your search text.

When you select an item from the list of search results, the Tell Me feature executes the relevant command and displays the resultant screen. In this way, the Tell Me feature helps you save the time it takes to locate a command on the ribbon. The Tell Me feature provides an option in the format **Get Help on "<keyword>"**, which will link to the online Visio Help content for the indicated keyword.

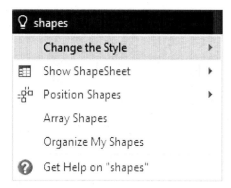

Figure 1-7: Keyword specified by using the Tell Me feature with the resultant screen.

| | **Note:** The Tell Me feature enables you to quickly access frequently searched commands by displaying the last five commands that were searched. |

| | Access the Checklist tile on your CHOICE Course screen for reference information and job aids on How to Use the Tell Me Feature. |

ACTIVITY 1–3
Customizing the Visio Drawing Interface

Data File
C:\091071Data\Getting Started with Visio 2016\B&B Phone Prospect Sales Process.vsdx

Before You Begin
The B&B Phone Prospect Sales Process.vsdx file is open.

Scenario
Now that you know more about the interface customization, you can modify some settings to help you work more efficiently.

---

1. Customize the status bar to add the PAN & ZOOM window.

    a) Move the pointer to the status bar and right-click.

    b) In the **Customize Status Bar** dialog box, observe the available options and check the **Pan & Zoom Window** check box.

Customize Status Bar	
✓ Page Number	1 of 1
✓ Width	
✓ Height	
✓ Length	
✓ Angle	
✓ Language	English (United States)
✓ Permissions	Off
✓ Macro Recording	Not Recording
✓ Upload Status	
✓ View Shortcuts	
✓ Zoom Slider	
✓ Zoom	100%
✓ Zoom to Fit	
✓ Pan & Zoom Window	
✓ Switch Windows	

Verify that the **Pan & Zoom Window** button ⊕ is now displayed on the **status bar**. *Right side after zoom %*

    c) Select the **Pan & Zoom Window** button.

    d) Try the zoom and pan functions.

e) Minimize the PAN & ZOOM window first by selecting the **AutoHide** pin (so that it is activated, and not turned off), and then move the pointer out of the window and into the center of the drawing.

Verify that the PAN & ZOOM window is minimized on the side of the **Drawing** page.

f) Expand the PAN & ZOOM window again by moving the pointer over it.

2. Customize the **Quick Access Toolbar** by adding the **Save As** button.

a) Select the **Customize Quick Access Toolbar** drop-down menu  on the right side of the **Quick Access Toolbar**.

b) Select **More Commands**.

c) Select **Save As** from the left pane.

d) Select **Add**.

Verify that **Save As** has moved to the right pane.

e) Select **OK** to save your changes and exit the **Visio Options** dialog box.

Verify that **Save As** is now displayed on the **Quick Access Toolbar**.

TOPIC B

Use Backstage Commands

The **Backstage** view, a common feature in many Windows programs since 2010, provides a way to access many essential commands that work "behind the scenes." A wealth of options exists here that can make your work more efficient, so it is worthwhile to spend some time exploring them. In this topic, you will use Backstage commands to customize Visio settings.

The Backstage View

The **Backstage** view is a separate part of the Visio 2016 interface dedicated to whole file and whole program operations. Just as the drawing interface contains a rich variety of tools and options, the **Backstage** view provides a convenient interface for whole file activities such as selecting a template, printing, saving, exporting, and more. It also holds a number of miscellaneous options, such as global Visio settings.

Components of the Backstage View

There are 11 tabs in the **Backstage** view, which together give access to hundreds of settings. When you start Visio, the **Backstage** view appears, with active tabs related to opening or creating a drawing, Office account settings, and global Visio settings. When you access the **Backstage** view from an open drawing, the tabs for whole file operations are also available.

Components of the
Backstage View

Ask students what Visio
tab they would use often
along with their reasons.

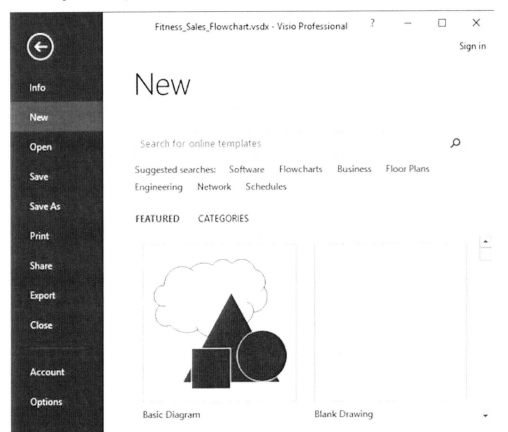

Figure 1–8: The Backstage view.

The tabs in the **Backstage** view are described in the following table.

Tab Name	Allows You To
Info	Manage file information, such as properties, Visio version compatibility, publishing options, and data connections for the current drawing.
New	Search for and select a template, and create a drawing.
Open	Navigate to the location of a Visio drawing and open it.
Save	Save an existing drawing.
Save As	Save a new drawing or save an existing drawing under a new name.
Print	Set printing options, adjust page setup, and preview a print.
Share	Share your drawing over the cloud or as an email attachment.
Export	Create a PDF/XPS document or change the drawing file type.
Close	Close the currently open file but leave Visio open.
Account	Select Office theme, sign in to Office, and view Visio product information.
Options	Access a rich palette of global Visio settings such as advanced interface customization options. Some of these customizations are also available on the main ribbon of the drawing interface.

The New Tab

In the **Backstage** view, the **New** tab is used for creating a new drawing. It provides an interactive screen for selecting your drawing template, which is the first step in creating a drawing.

ACTIVITY 1-4
Working with Visio 2016 Global Options

Before You Begin
The B&B Phone Prospect Sales Process.vsdx file is open.

Scenario
Now that you know more about the elements of a Visio drawing, you want to take a closer look at the whole file options on the **File** tab. You would also like to navigate the printing options.

1. Examine the global options.
   a) In the **B&B Phone Prospect Sales Process.vsdx** file, select the **File** tab.
   b) In the **Backstage** view, verify that the **Info** tab is selected.

2. Add a comment.
   a) Locate the **Properties** column on the right side.
   b) Locate the **Comments** field.
   c) Select the **Add comments** text box and type *Under Review by Marketing*
   d) Select anywhere outside the comment field to finalize it.

Properties ▾

Content Type	Microsoft Visio Drawing
Size	40.1 Kb (41,050 bytes)
Template	BASFLO_U.VSTX
Company	Specify the company
Categories	Add a category
Title	Add a title
Subject	Specify the subject
Tags	Add a tag
Comments	Under Review by Marketing

3. Change the paper orientation and keep the file open.
   a) In the **Backstage** view, select the **Print** tab.
   b) Change the paper orientation from **Landscape** to **Portrait** and then back to **Landscape**.
   c) Leave the file open.

TOPIC C

Save a File

As you progress in developing your drawing, you will need to save your work. The **Save** command allows you to save a new drawing in the current Visio format or in an older version format, and you can also save a drawing as a graphic in one of the many formats available. In this topic, you will save a file in multiple file formats.

Legacy Files

It is likely that you will encounter Visio files created in previous versions (2003, 2007, or 2010), or you may be collaborating with colleagues who are still using a previous version. In some cases, you will want to update these files to the new format, whereas in other cases you may want to ensure that any changes you make will be compatible with the previous version. Visio 2016 can handle both situations.

Compatibility Mode

When you open a file created in a previous Visio version (2003–2010), Compatibility Mode is automatically invoked, and appears in the title bar to the right of the file name. In this mode, certain Visio 2016 capabilities, such as new themes and styles, are disabled, so that you can't accidentally add them to a legacy file, which is a file created in a previous version of the software. When you save the file, you can choose the older format type.

File Saving Formats

There are two main file saving formats in Visio 2016: the native *VSDX* format and the legacy VSD drawing format. By default, Visio 2016 drawings use the VSDX format, which is based upon *Open Packaging Conventions (OPC)* and *Extensible Markup Language (XML)*. The formats for versions of Visio prior to Visio 2013 were the Visio binary file format (*VSD*), or the Visio XML Drawing file format. The VSDX format has many advantages, such as a smaller file size, less vulnerability to file corruption, and greater ability to be modified by third-party software.

Compatibility Checker

You may want to tell students that a Visio 2016 file is similar to a ZIP container in that it is actually a collection of files. For example, each page has its own part, and each master shape has its own part.

Whenever you save a new drawing in the legacy **VSD** drawing format, a **Compatibility Check** dialog box is displayed. This dialog box lists the details of the new features that will be down-converted and the number of such occurrences in your document. You then have a chance to cancel the save if you don't want to lose these features.

Other File Saving Type Options

A Visio drawing is made of multiple components, such as stencils, templates, and shapes. You can save these particular components of a drawing file by selecting one of these type options from the **Save As** dialog box. You can also save a drawing in one of many image formats, such as PNG, BMP, and JPG, as well as other file options such as PDF and XPS.

File Saving Locations

Visio 2016 gives you many options for file saving locations: local computer or, if you are connected online, *OneDrive* and *Microsoft Office 365* SharePoint. Connecting and saving to the cloud offers many advantages over saving on a local device, such as accessibility from any connected computer or other device, and larger storage capacity.

Note: For more information, check out the LearnTO **Save Your Visio Files to the Cloud** presentation from the **LearnTO** tile on the CHOICE Course screen.

You may want to show LearnTO **Save Your Visio Files to the Cloud** from the CHOICE Course screen or have students navigate out to the Course screen and watch it themselves as a supplement to your instruction. If not, please remind students to visit the LearnTOs for this course on their CHOICE Course screen after class for supplemental information and additional resources.

 Access the Checklist tile on your CHOICE Course screen for reference information and job aids on How to Save Files.

ACTIVITY 1-5
Saving a Visio Drawing

Before You Begin

The B&B Phone Prospect Sales Process.vsdx file is open.

Scenario

You edited the Sales flow chart by adding a comment. Now you'd like to save it to your local computer. You would also like to save the file in the previous Visio format to show to a colleague who has Visio 2010 on her system. In addition, you are curious about the Compatibility Checker.

---

1. Save the file on your local computer in the Visio 2016 file format (VSDX).

   a) With the **B&B Phone Prospect Sales Process.vsdx** file open, access the **Backstage** view.

    Note: If the drawing interface is displayed, select the **File** tab first.

   b) From the **Backstage** view, select **Save As**.
   c) Select **Browse**. Navigate to **C:\091071Data\Getting Started with Visio 2016** and save the file with the default file type, naming it *My B&B Phone Prospect Sales Process.vsdx*
   d) Select **Save** to complete the save operation.

2. Save the file on your local computer, in the 2003-2010 Visio file format (VSD), using the Compatibility Checker tool.

   a) With the **B&B Phone Prospect Sales Process.vsdx** file open, access the **Backstage**.

    Note: If the drawing interface is displayed, select the **File** tab first.

   b) From the **Backstage** view, select **Save As**.
   c) Select **Browse** and navigate to **C:\091071Data\Getting Started with Visio 2016**.
   d) From the **Save as type** drop-down list, select **Visio 2003-2010 Drawing (*.vsd)**.
   e) In the **File name** text box, type *My 2010 B&B Phone Prospect Sales Process Legacy.vsd*
   f) Select **Save**.
   g) In the **Microsoft Visio Compatibility Checker** dialog box, note the summary of what will change (shadow effect and theme effects) and the number of occurrences.

h) Select **Continue** to save the document.

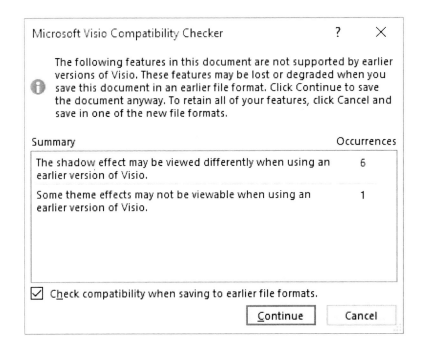

i) Close the file.

Summary

In this lesson, you performed some basic tasks in Visio 2016, such as navigating the drawing interface, identifying drawing components, and exploring the ribbon commands. While performing these tasks, you gained some familiarity with the components of the Visio interface. Also, you used the **Backstage** view and saved a Visio drawing to the cloud and to your local computer in a legacy version, too. All these skills have given you a foundation to build upon as you prepare for the next step, which is to create a Visio drawing.

Encourage students to use the social networking tools provided on the CHOICE Course screen to follow up with their peers after the course is completed for further discussion and resources to support continued learning.

How might your experience in other Microsoft applications be applicable to Visio 2016? What aspects of Visio are similar to these applications? What differences do you see?

A: Answers will vary, but interface items such as the ribbon, status bar, Quick Access Toolbar, and others may be mentioned as similarities.

Can you think of any current or past tasks that Visio could help you perform, either at work or at home?

A: Answers will vary, but will probably include floor plans, work process diagrams, and maps.

Note: Check your CHOICE Course screen for opportunities to interact with your classmates, peers, and the larger CHOICE online community about the topics covered in this course or other topics you are interested in. From the Course screen you can also access available resources for a more continuous learning experience.

2 | Working with Workflow Diagram Tools

Lesson Time: 1 hour

Lesson Objectives

In this lesson, you will work with various workflow diagram tools. You will:

- Use drawing components such as templates, stencils, shapes, and text.
- Modify a drawing.
- Insert callouts and groups.

Lesson Introduction

Now that you've navigated the drawing interface and the **Backstage** view, customized the interface to suit your preferences, and observed the components of a drawing, it's time to create a drawing. Here, you will create a workflow diagram by using Visio's features to work with shapes, text, and connectors. In this lesson, you will work with various workflow diagram tools.

TOPIC A

Use Drawing Components

Now that you understand how the components of a drawing fit together, you will focus on using templates, stencils, and shapes in preparation for creating your drawing. In this topic, you will use drawing components and text.

Template Selection

Template Selection

Before you create a new drawing, the first step is to select a template by using the **New** tab in the **Backstage** view. You can select a template from a set of featured templates, search according to categories, or even search from Microsoft's online Visio collection.

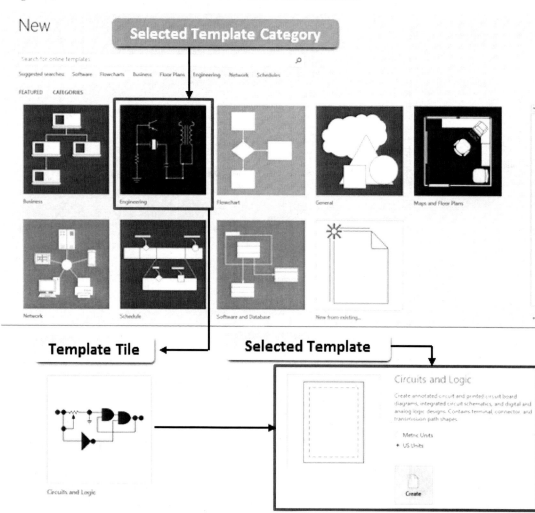

Figure 2-1: The Engineering template selected in the Startup screen.

The template categories are:

- Business
- Engineering
- Flowchart
- General

- Maps and Floor Plans
- Network
- Schedule
- Software and Database

Some categories contain only two templates, while others contain dozens. The **Maps and Floor Plans** category in Visio 2016 includes modernized shapes for Office Layouts, detailed shapes for Site Plans, updated shapes for Floor Plans, and modern shapes for Home Plans. The enhancements to these diagrams are some of the new features of Visio 2016.

	Note: For the complete list of new features included in Visio 2016, see **https:// support.office.com/en-us/article/What-s-new-in-Visio-2016-798f4f39-2833-486b-9ae9-55162672102e**.
	Note: You can use the **New from existing** option in the **CATEGORIES** section to create a new Visio drawing based on an existing Visio drawing.
	Note: For more information, check out the LearnTO **Search for a Template Online** presentation from the **LearnTO** tile on the CHOICE Course screen.

Starter Diagrams

Starter diagrams refer to the built-in diagrams of Visio 2016, which provide suitable layouts according to the template category. You can use these layouts to build your diagram easily without having to start from scratch with a blank template every time. When you create your diagram from a starter diagram, the **Drawing** page will contain a readable replica of the layout, related stencil shapes, and a tip pane. You can modify the layout by selecting suitable shapes from the stencil. The tip pane is displayed at one of the ends of the diagram and indicates the possible actions you can perform with the current diagram.

You may want to show LearnTO **Search for a Template Online** from the CHOICE Course screen or have students navigate out to the Course screen and watch it themselves as a supplement to your instruction. If not, please remind students to visit the LearnTOs for this course on their CHOICE Course screen after class for supplemental information and additional resources.

Starter Diagrams

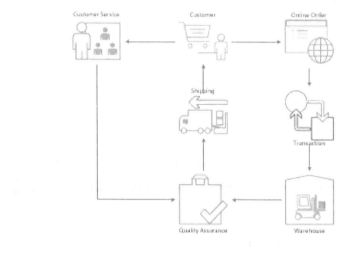

Figure 2–2: Initial output of Department Workflow starter diagram with the Tips pane.

Note: Starter diagrams are available only for specific categories. Further, you must remove the tip pane from the diagram before finalizing it.

Stencil and Shape Management

Stencil and Shape
Management

When the drawing is created, the stencils included in the template are all open in the Shapes window, but only the active stencil is highlighted. The inactive stencils are stacked on top of each other. You need to activate a stencil by selecting its title bar and use the options in the title bar to close the stencil.

Sometimes you may need to use shapes that are not included in the template's stencils. You can add additional stencils by using the **More Shapes** option at the top of the Shapes window, which allows you to access the template categories and drill down to select a stencil, which will be loaded into the Shapes window.

You can search for individual shapes by name from the **Search** pane in the Shapes window. This search checks through shapes installed with Visio, or on the Microsoft website, when you are connected to the Internet. Once you find the desired shape, you can open its stencil and add it to the stencils in your Shapes window, or add the individual shape to your **Favorites** stencil.

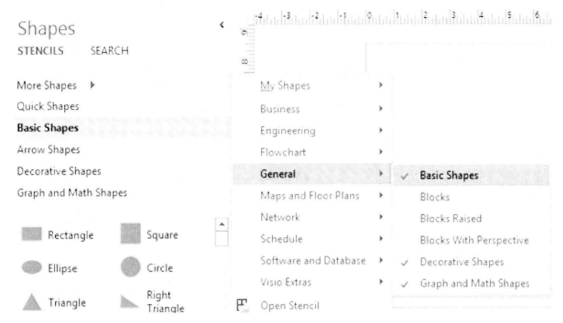

Figure 2-3: The More Shapes option.

Favorites Stencil

Switching between many stencils to select shapes can be cumbersome. One solution is to collect the shapes you use most often into the *Favorites stencil*. The **Favorites** stencil is created automatically when you install Visio and is located in **More Shapes→My Shapes**. You can also store shapes you've found in searches here, as well as any shapes you've modified or created.

 Note: For more information, check out the LearnTO **Search for a Shape Online** presentation from the **LearnTO** tile on the CHOICE Course screen.

 Access the Checklist tile on your CHOICE Course screen for reference information and job aids on How to Select a Template.

You may want to show LearnTO **Search for a Shape Online** from the CHOICE Course screen or have students navigate out to the Course screen and watch it themselves as a supplement to your instruction. If not, please remind students to visit the LearnTOs for this course on their CHOICE Course screen after class for supplemental information and additional resources.

ACTIVITY 2-1
Creating a File from a Template

Before You Begin
Visio is open but no drawing files are open.

Scenario
B&B Fitness has decided to implement an interactive voice response (IVR) system to handle incoming phone calls. Your manager has asked you make a diagram of the proposed workflow for a preliminary meeting with a third-party IVR supplier. Because you are new to Visio, you want to explore the template selection and find an appropriate one for your assignment. Then you want to create a file and save it.

1. Select the template category.
   a) In the Visio window, select the **File** tab.
   b) In the **Backstage** view, verify that **New** is selected, and select **CATEGORIES**.
   c) Select **Flowchart**.
   d) Select **Basic Flowchart**.

2. Use a template with a starter diagram.
   a) Select the first starter diagram, **Vertical Flowchart**, which is to the right of the blank template.
      View the description of the template, layout of the flowchart, and the contents of the **TIP** section.
   b) Select **Create**.
   c) Use the zoom controls in the status bar to zoom the drawing to 100 percent. Read the tip pane on the left of the Drawing page.
   d) Select **File→Close**.

3. Start a new file.
   a) Select the **File** tab.
   b) Select **CATEGORIES**.
   c) Select **Flowchart**.
   d) Select **Basic Flowchart**.

4. Select the Basic Flowchart template and scroll through the drawing.
   a) Select the blank template, **Basic Flowchart**, and verify that the template description for the blank template is displayed.
      View the template description for the blank template and the note in the **TIP** section.
   b) Verify that **US Units** is selected. Select **Create** to make a drawing and view the **Drawing Interface**.
      Verify that the Shapes window is populated with the **Basic Flowchart Shapes** stencil, which is active as indicated by the highlighted title bar, and the **Cross-Functional Flowchart Shapes** stencil, which has only its title bar displayed.
   c) Scroll through the **Basic Flowchart Shapes**.

5. Close the **Cross-Functional Flowchart Shapes** stencil.
   a) Right-click the title bar of the **Cross-Functional Flowchart Shapes** stencil and select **Close** from the menu.

6. Save the file.
   a) On the **Quick Access Toolbar**, select **Save As**.

b) Navigate to C:\091071Data\Working with Workflow Diagram Tools.
c) Name the file *My IVR Phone Process* and save it as a **Visio Drawing** (*.vsdx).
d) Select **Save** and leave the file open.

> **Access the Checklist tile on your CHOICE Course screen for reference information and job aids on How to Manage Stencils and Shapes.**

Types of Connectors

The default connector on the ribbon allows you to connect one shape with another individual shape because it supports only one-to-one connection. The **Connector** stencil contains other connector types that allow you to connect a single shape to multiple shapes. By default, the **One to many** connector allows you to connect a single shape to a maximum of three shapes. Similarly, both the **Multi-tree sloped** and the **Multi-tree square** connectors allow you to connect a single shape to a maximum of six shapes.

Connection Points

Connection points are special types of points to which you can glue connectors and shapes. These points are available only for some shapes. The connection points ensure that the glued connectors continue to be connected even when the shape is moved. Most shapes have only one connection point on each side.

The **Connection Point** tool on the **Home** tab allows you to create your own connection points. Further, you can move connection points by dragging them with the **Connection Point** tool. In addition, the **Connection Point** tool allows you to remove connection points.

Types of Connection Points

Visio 2016 supports three types of connection points: Inward, Outward, or Inward & Outward.

Connection Point	Used When
Inward	2-D shapes need to attract the endpoints on connectors and the other types of connection points. This type is used most of the time.
Outward	2-D shapes need to be glued to another shape. This type connects to an inward connection point.
Inward & Outward	A shape is available but you don't know how it needs to be glued to other shapes.

Types of Connection Points

Point vs. Dynamic Connections

Connections can be made to a specific connection point on a shape (point connection) or to the shape as a whole (dynamic connection). Point connections always preserve the same connection points when shapes are moved, which sometimes results in a complicated connector path. Dynamic connections can readjust the location of the connection on the shape's edge to create a more direct connection path.

Point vs. Dynamic Connections

The easiest way to make connections is with **AutoConnect** activated on the **View** tab, in the **Visual Aids** group. When a shape is dragged over an existing shape or selected from the **Quick Shapes** mini toolbar and then released over one of the **AutoConnect** triangles, the new shape will be connected automatically in a shape-to-shape connection to the existing shape.

By using the **Connector** tool, you can also insert connectors manually, by *gluing* the begin point to a connection point on the first shape, and dragging the end point to a connection point on the second shape. You can also create shape-to-shape connections by using this tool, as long as the entire shape is highlighted when the connection is made.

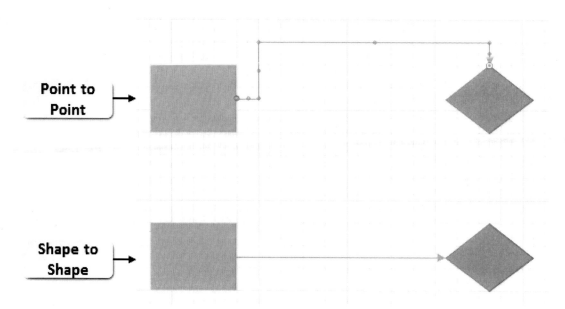

Figure 2–4: Connector types.

Connector's Path

The connector's path is chosen automatically to avoid other shapes when possible, and line jumps show where connectors cross over each other. If needed, you can also control the connector's path by using handles that appear when a connector is selected, and there are settings to control the style of connector: straight line, right-angle segments, or curved.

Dynamic Grid

Dynamic Grid

The **Dynamic Grid** on the **View** tab, in the **Visual Aids** group, facilitates consistent spacing and alignment of shapes by providing alignment guides that appear as you drag a shape near an existing shape or next to a page margin:

- Center alignment: Displayed when the centers of shapes are aligned.
- Edge alignment: Displayed when shapes of different sizes align along their top or bottom edges.
- Spacing alignment: Displayed when the spacing matches the default spacing or when it matches the space between other nearby shapes.

When the *Dynamic Grid* is activated, shapes dropped near a guide will *snap* into place. Snapping pulls shapes to ruler subdivisions, grid lines, guides, or guide points so that you do not have to place a shape in the exact position manually. You can also control the **Snap and Glue** settings with options accessed from the **View** tab, in the **Visual Aids** group dialog box launcher.

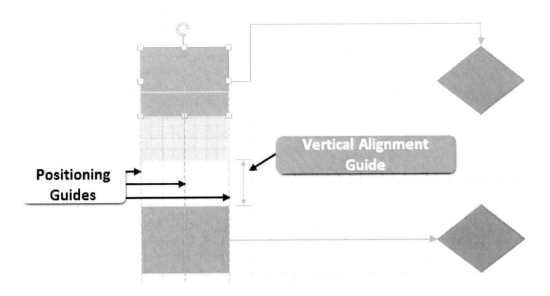

Figure 2-5: The dynamic grid displayed on selecting a shape.

 Access the Checklist tile on your CHOICE Course screen for reference information and job aids on How to Add Shapes and Connectors to a Drawing.

Need for Including Text in Shapes and Connectors

Text is an important part of any diagram. Visio allows you to label both shapes and connectors with text, and also lets you create free-standing text. By adding text to shapes and connectors, you will be able to describe the steps in a diagram or provide other important information. There is a full palette of text commands on the **Home** tab contained in the **Font** and **Paragraph** groups, and text can be rotated and moved just like any other drawing element.

The Text Dialog Box

The *Text dialog box* allows you to apply additional formatting options, such as transparency, spacing, margins, and background color, that are not available by default on the ribbon. The dialog box launcher in the **Font** or **Paragraph** groups allows you to access the **Text** dialog box.

The Text Dialog Box

The **Text** dialog box contains six tabs, as described in the following table.

Tab	Allows You To
Font	Change font styles, such as font face, size, style, color, casing, and transparency.
Character	Set character spacing and scaling.
Paragraph	Set paragraph alignment, spacing, and indentation.
Text Block	Set margins, alignment, background color, and background transparency.
Tabs	Define the position and alignment of tab stops in text blocks.

Tab	Allows You To
Bullets	Select bullet styles and related options.

 Access the Checklist tile on your CHOICE Course screen for reference information and job aids on How to Add and Edit Text.

Drawing Shortcuts

Drawing Shortcuts

Here are some useful keyboard shortcuts to use when creating or modifying a drawing.

Action	Press
Open the **Home** tab in the ribbon.	**Alt+H**
Open the **Text** dialog box.	**F11**
Open the **Format Shape** task pane.	**F3**
Move from shape to shape on the **Drawing** page. A dotted rectangle indicates the shape that has the focus.	**Tab**
Note: You cannot move to shapes that are protected against selection or on a locked layer.	
Move from shape to shape on the **Drawing** page in reverse order.	**Shift+Tab**
Select a shape that has focus.	**Enter**
Note: To select multiple shapes, press the **Tab** key to bring focus to the first shape you want to select, and then press **Enter**. Hold down **Shift** while you press the **Tab** key to bring focus to another shape. When the focus rectangle is over the shape you want, press **Enter** to add that shape to the selection. Repeat for each shape you want to select.	
Clear selection of or focus on a shape.	**Esc**
Switch between text edit mode and shape selection mode on a selected shape.	**F2**
Nudge a selected shape.	Arrow keys
Nudge a selected shape one pixel at a time.	**Shift**+arrow keys
Note: Scroll Lock must be turned off.	

 Note: For a complete list of keyboard shortcuts, see **office.microsoft.com/en-us/visio-help/ keyboard-shortcuts-for-visio-HA102748913.aspx?CTT=1** or go to **office.microsoft.com** and search for Visio keyboard shortcuts.

ACTIVITY 2-2
Working with Shapes and Text

Before You Begin
The file My IVR Phone Process.vsdx is open.

Scenario
Your first idea for the IVR workflow is to have incoming calls routed through the IVR to three departments: training, operator, and billing. You want to put your ideas into a Visio drawing to help you conceptualize them. You've already created and saved the file. Now you want to populate it with shapes.

1. Verify the setup of your drawing interface settings.

   Design, Orientation Portrait

   a) On the **View** tab, in the **Visual Aids** group, verify that the **Dynamic Grid** and **Connection Points** check boxes are checked. If necessary, check the **AutoConnect** check box.
   b) On the **View** tab, in the **Show** group, verify that the **Ruler** check box is checked and check the **Grid** check box.
   c) On the **Home** tab, in the **Tools** group, verify that the **Pointer** tool is selected.
   d) In the Shapes window, verify that the **Basic Flowchart Shapes** stencil is active.

2. Place the first shape in the drawing.
   a) Zoom in to about 75 percent by using the **Zoom** slider on the status bar.
   b) Drag the **Start/End** shape to the **Drawing** page. Locate it along the left side of the screen of its selection box at (1,5) where the first number is on the horizontal ruler and the second is on the vertical. Then release it.
   c) Select anywhere outside of the shape to finalize it.

3. Add text to the shape.
   a) Double-click in the center of the shape.

      Observe that an automatic zoom is displayed when you double-click the shape.
   b) Type *Incoming Call*
   c) Select anywhere outside of the shape to exit the text mode and create the text.

	Note: You may need to zoom in again as you work.

4. Add the next shape by using **AutoConnect**.
   a) Select the **Incoming Call** shape.
   b) Locate the pointer over the center of the **Incoming Call** shape.

      Verify that the **AutoConnect** arrows are displayed in four directions.
   c) Carefully move toward the right arrow.

      Verify the contents of the mini shapes toolbar.

d) Carefully move the pointer over the **Process** (rectangle) shape on the Quick Shapes mini toolbar.

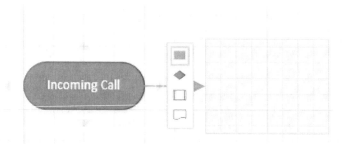

 Note: The preview will show the shape in place.

e) Select the **Process** shape.

 Note: At this point, the shape is highlighted for resizing or rotation.

f) Move the pointer over the middle of the shape, double-click, and type the text *IVR System* on the shape.

g) Select anywhere outside the shape to exit the **Text Editing** mode and automatically zoom out.

Verify that the rectangle has been placed one-half inch to the right of the **Incoming Call** shape, with its center aligned vertically with the center of that shape.

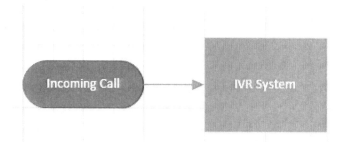

 Note: A connector was added automatically with its start point on the first shape and its end point (arrow head) on the second shape, resulting in a shape-to-shape connection.

Ask the students to verify that the **Data** shape is not one of the first four shapes in the **Basic Flowchart Shapes** stencil and therefore does not appear in the **Quick Shapes** mini toolbar. Mention that another option here would be to simply move the Data shape up in the Quick Shapes area so that it is one of the top four shapes, which would automatically appear in the Quick Shapes mini toolbar.

Ask the students to verify that the parallelogram has been placed one-half inch above the **IVR System** shape, with its center aligned horizontally with the center of the previous shape, and that it is dynamically connected to the **IVR System** shape by an arrow.

5. Modify the text in the second shape to use italics.
   a) Select the second shape (IVR System).
   b) Select the **Home** tab.
   c) In the **Font** group, select the **Italic** button.
   d) Select anywhere on the page to finalize the modification.

6. Place a data shape above the **IVR System** shape.
   a) Select the **Data** shape or parallelogram in the **Basic Flowchart Shapes** stencil and carefully drag it over the IVR System shape, moving slowly upward and past the shape until the top **AutoConnect** arrow is highlighted, and then release it.
   b) While the shape handles are highlighted, type *Add caller to DB* and select anywhere outside the shape to finalize it in the drawing.

7. Place another three shapes, this time without a connection, as you will add a special connector in a later step.

a) On the **View** tab, in the **Visual Aids** group, uncheck the **AutoConnect** check box.
b) Drag and place a **Process** shape from the stencil to the right of the **IVR System** shape.
c) When the horizontal green alignment guides appear below the shape, release the shape.
d) Label it as *Operator*
   Verify that it is one-half inch to the right of the **IVR System** shape.
e) Drag another **Process** shape from the stencil and locate it above the **Operator** shape.
f) When the first vertical green alignment guide appears, release the shape.
g) Label it as *Billing*
h) Drag another process shape from the stencil and locate it below the **Operator** shape.
i) When the vertical green alignment guides appear, release the shape.
j) Label it as *Training*

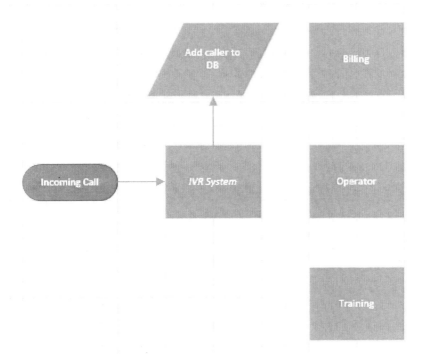

8. Add a **One to many** connector shape to the **Favorites** stencil.

    Note: This connector works well for up to three shapes from one stem. To connect even more shapes, you can use one of the multi-tree connectors.

   a) From the Shapes window, select **More Shapes→Visio Extras→Connectors**.
   b) Select the **Connectors** stencil.
   c) Scroll down to find the **One to many** connector.
   d) Right-click the connector and select **Add to My Shapes→Favorites**.
   e) Select **More Shapes→My Shapes→Favorites** and select **Favorites** so that a checkmark appears next to it.

    Note: The **Favorites** stencil is loaded to the **Shapes** window and is active.

   f) Close the **Connectors** stencil by right-clicking on its title bar and selecting **Close**.

9. Add a one to many connector to your diagram.
   a) If necessary, select the title bar of the **Favorites** stencil to make it the active stencil.

b) Drag the **One to many** connector to the **Drawing** page and drop it between the **IVR System** shape and the **Operator** shape.

10. Resize and connect the **One to many** connector to the **IVR System**, **Billing**, **Operator**, and **Training** shapes with point-to-point connections.

a) Drag the left connection point of the **One to many** connector to the connector in the middle of the right side of the **IVR System** shape and release it.

b) Drag the end connection point of the top branch of the **One to many** connector to the connection point in the middle of the left side of the **Billing** shape and release it.

c) Drag the end connection point of the middle branch of the **One to many** connector to the connection point in the middle of the left side of the **Operator** shape and release it.

d) Drag the end connection point of the bottom branch of the **One to many** connector to the connection point in the middle of the left side of the **Training** shape and release it.

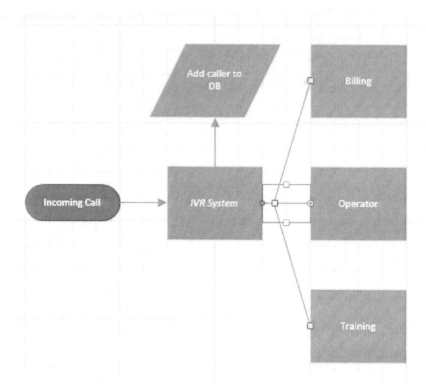

e) Save the drawing by selecting the **Save** button on the **Quick Access Toolbar**.

f) Close the file by selecting **File→Close**.

Summary

In this lesson, you performed some basic tasks in Visio 2016, such as navigating the drawing interface, identifying drawing components, and exploring the ribbon commands. While performing these tasks, you gained some familiarity with the components of the Visio interface. Also, you used the **Backstage** view and saved a Visio drawing to the cloud and to your local computer in a legacy version, too. All these skills have given you a foundation to build upon as you prepare for the next step, which is to create a Visio drawing.

How might your experience in other Microsoft applications be applicable to Visio 2016? What aspects of Visio are similar to these applications? What differences do you see?

A: Answers will vary, but interface items such as the ribbon, status bar, Quick Access Toolbar, and others may be mentioned as similarities.

Encourage students to use the social networking tools provided on the CHOICE Course screen to follow up with their peers after the course is completed for further discussion and resources to support continued learning.

Can you think of any current or past tasks that Visio could help you perform, either at work or at home?

A: Answers will vary, but will probably include floor plans, work process diagrams, and maps.

 Note: Check your CHOICE Course screen for opportunities to interact with your classmates, peers, and the larger CHOICE online community about the topics covered in this course or other topics you are interested in. From the Course screen you can also access available resources for a more continuous learning experience.

TOPIC B

Modify a Drawing

As much as you'd like to create a perfect drawing in one session, changes are inevitable, whether driven by your own refinements or in response to the feedback of stakeholders. Visio has a full array of tools to help you modify, move, and align shapes, text, and connectors. In this topic, you will modify a drawing.

SIZE & POSITION Window

SIZE & POSITION Window

The SIZE & POSITION window allows you to control how and where the objects are placed on the **Drawing** page. The fields of the SIZE & POSITION window are described in the table.

Field	Allows You to Set
X	The position of the point along the horizontal or top ruler. For some shapes, which do not have a square or a rectangular outline selection, this field will be replaced by two fields, **Begin X** and **End X**.
Y	The position of the point along the vertical or left ruler. For some shapes, which do not have a square or a rectangular outline selection, this field will be replaced by two fields, **Begin Y** and **End Y**.
Width	The width of the selected shape.
Height	The height of the selected shape.
Angle	The angle of rotation of the selected shape.
Pin Pos	The position of the shape based on the pin position, Pin Pos, in short. You can modify the Pin Pos by selecting the desired position from the drop-down list.

Shapes and Connectors Selection Methods

Visio provides many methods to select shapes and connectors for modification. With the **Area Select** tool, you need to drag a rectangle to select all shapes within it. With the **Lasso Select** tool, you need to drag a free form shape around the items you want to select. With either method, the selected items can also be moved, rotated, or resized as a group by using the appropriate handles.

> Access the Checklist tile on your CHOICE Course screen for reference information and job aids on How to Modify Shapes.

Alignment Options

Alignment Options

Visio allows you to align the objects of your drawing by using the **Align Shapes** option in the **Arrange** group of the **Home** tab. You can use the **Auto Align** option to automatically align the selected object to the grid of the drawing. You can adjust the alignment of the selected object to the left, center, or right of the grid.

Also, you can use the other alignment options to align an object with respect to a primary object. You can align the second object to the left, center, right, top, middle, or bottom of the primary object.

Figure 2-6: The Align options in the Arrange group.

 Access the Checklist tile on your CHOICE Course screen for reference information and job aids on How to Modify the Alignment.

ACTIVITY 2–3
Modifying a Drawing

Data File
C:\091071Data\Working with Workflow Diagram Tools\B&B Phone Prospect Sales Process.vsdx

Scenario
You are planning to incorporate the **B&B Phone Prospect Sales Process** diagram into the IVR diagram you've been working on. To prepare it for integration into the diagram, you review it and decide to make the following changes:

- Enlarge the **Inbound Phone prospect** shape so that it is 1.5 inches wide.
- Redo the connections to **Trial membership buy-in** to make sure they are shape-to-shape, because the shapes they are connected to may end up being moved later.
- Replace the document shape with a database shape.

Here is the result of these changes:

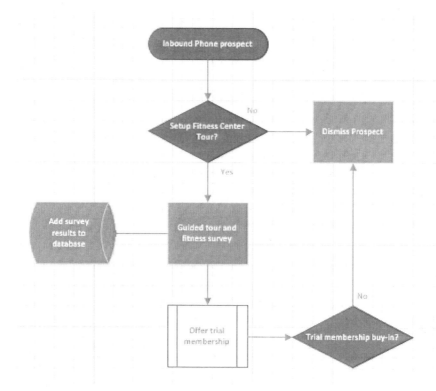

1. Open the file **B&B Phone Prospect Sales Process.vsdx**.
   a) Navigate to the **C:\091071Data\Working with Workflow Diagram Tools** folder.
   b) Select the file **B&B Phone Prospect Sales Process.vsdx** and open it.
   c) On the **View** tab, in the **Visual Aids** group, uncheck the **AutoConnect** check box.

2. Enlarge the **Inbound Phone prospect** shape.
   a) Select the **Inbound Phone prospect** shape.

Verify that the selection handles are displayed and the current width dimension in the status bar is 1 inch.

b) Select the handle in the middle of the right side and stretch the shape until the width reaches 1.5 inches.

Verify that the connector to the decision shape is no longer straight.

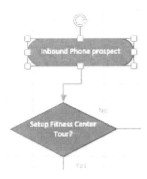

c) Realign the **Inbound Phone prospect** shape by dragging it to the left so that it is centered over the diamond shape until the alignment guide for center lines appears; then release it.

Verify that the connector is now straight.

3. Delete the connectors to **Trial membership buy-in**.

a) Select the connector between the **Trial membership buy-in** and the **Dismiss Prospect** shapes.

Verify that the selection handles are displayed.

b) Press **Delete**.

c) Select the connector between the **Offer trial membership** and **Trial membership buy-in** shapes.

d) Right-click and select **Cut**.

4. Redo the connectors to **Trial membership buy-in** so they are shape-to-shape.

a) On the **Home** tab, in the **Tools** group, select **Connector**.

Verify that the cursor symbol changes to a + icon .

b) Hover the cursor over the middle of the **Offer trial membership** shape until the entire shape is highlighted.

c) Drag a connector to the middle of **Trial membership buy-in** until the entire shape is highlighted, or a **Glue to Shape** tool tip appears.

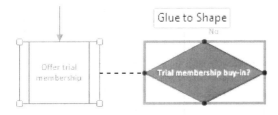

> Mention to the students that in step 3, the **Cut** command is used as an alternate method to delete the connector and so is not followed by a **Paste** command. Normally, the **Cut** command will be followed by the **Paste** command to move the contents.

d) Release the mouse button.

5. Repeat steps 4b and 4c to create a new shape-to-shape connector between **Trial membership buy-in** and **Dismiss Prospect**.

6. Replace the **Document** shape with a **Database** shape.

a) On the **Home** tab, in the **Tools** group, select the **Pointer** tool.

b) Select the **Document** shape labeled **Add survey results to Database**.

c) On the **Home** tab, in the **Editing** group, select **Change Shape**.

    d) Point to the **Database** shape, 3D horizontal cylinder, and observe the live preview.

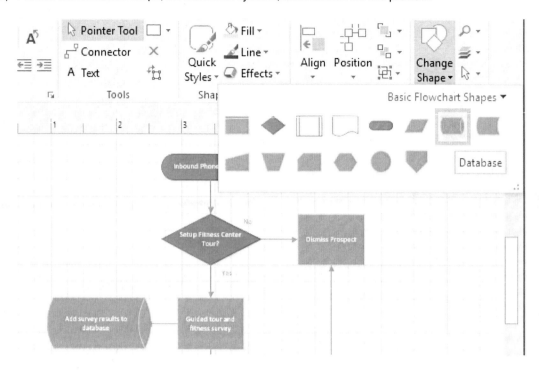

    e) Select the **Database** shape.

       Verify that the new shape has replaced the previous shape in the diagram.

    f) Select anywhere on the **Drawing** page to finalize it.

7. Reduce the size of the **Database** shape by using the **SIZE & POSITION** task pane.

    a) Select the database shape in the drawing.

    b) On the **View** tab, in the **Show** group, from the **Task Panes** drop-down menu, select **Size & Position**.

    c) In the **SIZE & POSITION** pane, select the **Width** field, type *1* and press **Enter**.

    d) Select anywhere on the **Drawing** page to finalize it.

    e) Select the **Close** button to close the **SIZE & POSITION** pane.

8. Save the file.

TOPIC C

Insert Callouts and Groups

As your diagram becomes more complex, you may need to perform operations on multiple shapes at once, both to save time and to maintain consistency. A more complex diagram may also need some explanatory text to convey the information more clearly. Visio has tools to meet the needs of complex diagrams. In this topic, you will insert callouts and groups.

Callouts

Many Visio drawings contain text in the form of labels on shapes (and optionally on connectors). If you need to convey more information about a shape, you could use a standalone text box, but there is no way to link it to a specific shape. Visio provides a more sophisticated solution, a callout, that will save you time and effort in creating, and later modifying, your drawing.

Callouts

A callout is a special annotation box that is associated with a shape. If the shape is moved, the callout will move with it; if the shape is copied or deleted, the callout will also be copied or deleted. When a callout is selected, you can see a yellow handle located on the center of the shape it is associated with.

There are a variety of style options for callouts, and the alignment can be easily adjusted by dragging the callout.

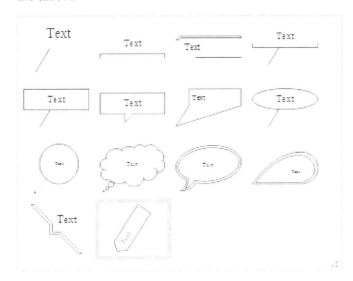

Figure 2-7: Callout styles with the Price Tag style selected.

 Note: Deleting a callout does not affect the shape it is associated with.

 Access the Checklist tile on your CHOICE Course screen for reference information and job aids on How to Create Callouts.

Groups

As your drawing becomes more complex, you may need to perform the same operation, such as moving or enlarging, on multiple shapes simultaneously. Visio's Group commands allow you to group shapes together to perform an operation, and then ungroup the shapes to treat each shape independently.

 Access the Checklist tile on your CHOICE Course screen for reference information and job aids on How to Use Grouping.

ACTIVITY 2-4
Inserting Callouts and Groups

Before You Begin
The file B&B Phone Prospect Sales Process.vsdx is open.

Scenario
In preparation for integrating the B&B Phone Prospect Sales Process diagram into the IVR diagram, you decide to add a callout, and also to place all of the shapes into a group so that it will be easier to position them in the IVR diagram.

1. Create a callout for the subprocess **Offer trial membership**.
   a) Select the subprocess **Offer trial membership**.
   b) On the **Insert** tab, in the **Diagram Parts** group, select **Callout**.
   c) Verify the various callout styles available. Hover the pointer over the second style in the top row to see a live preview.

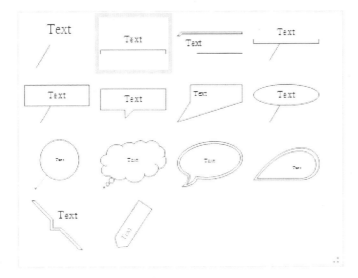

d) Select the style and the callout will be placed in the drawing, in selection mode, in the upper right of the shape, which is not a good location.

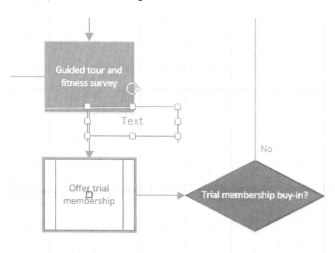

e) Drag the callout to the left side of the subprocess **Offer trial membership** and align it with the center of the shape by using the guidelines.

f) Select the callout and type the text *1 month unlimited use, 3 personal training sessions*

g) Select outside of the text editing box to create the callout.

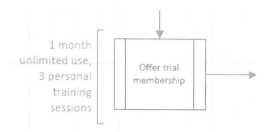

2. To make the callout stand out more, you decide to change the text font color to red.

a) Select the callout you just created.

b) On the **Home** tab, in the **Font** group, select the font color icon image and select the second red color in the Standard Colors.

You can point out that when you select a callout, a yellow handle appears on the center of the shape it is associated with.

3. Create a group from the entire drawing.

a) Select anywhere on the **Drawing** page, but not on any element.

b) Press **Ctrl + A** to select the entire drawing.

c) On the **Home** tab, in the **Arrange** group, select [⊞] Group ▾ (Group)→Group.

Verify that the shapes are now in a group, surrounded by the selection rectangle.

4. Modify the font style so all text is in italics.

   a) On the **Home** tab, in the **Font** group, select the italic I.

   b) Select only the callout, and remove the italics by toggling the italic I.

 Note: If necessary, ungroup the shapes in the drawing.

5. Save the file.

   a) On the **Quick Access Toolbar**, select the **Save As** button.

   b) Navigate to C:\091071Data\Working with Workflow Diagram Tools.

   c) Name the file *Modified B&B Phone Prospect Sales Process* and save the file as a **Visio Drawing (*.vsdx).**

   d) Close the file.

Summary

In this lesson, you created a new workflow diagram in Visio 2016 using the diagram components provided by Visio. You modified both the elements and the alignment of an existing flowchart diagram by using the built-in tools. Further, you inserted callouts that described the diagrams and organized multiple shapes into groups to handle the objects easily. Thus, you have used the essential commands to create and modify a drawing, but there are many more options in the ribbon menus that you will certainly explore as you become more proficient with Visio. In the following lessons, you will build on your knowledge of different types of Visio drawings, and use the specialized commands that are required for each type.

Encourage students to use the social networking tools provided on the CHOICE Course screen to follow up with their peers after the course is completed for further discussion and resources to support continued learning.

Which template categories do you think you will use most in your place of business? At home?

A: Answers will vary, but may include business, flowchart, maps and floor plans, or network.

How easy did you find it to modify an existing drawing in Visio? How does this compare with the process of modifying other products that you create with other Office software?

A: Answers will vary, but may include similarities to modifying a slide in PowerPoint or changing text appearance in Word.

 Note: Check your CHOICE Course screen for opportunities to interact with your classmates, peers, and the larger CHOICE online community about the topics covered in this course or other topics you are interested in. From the Course screen you can also access available resources for a more continuous learning experience.

3 Building Organization Charts

Lesson Time: 1 hour, 15 minutes

Lesson Objectives

In this lesson, you will build organization charts. You will:

- Create an organization chart manually.

- Create organization charts by using the starter diagrams and the Organization Chart Wizard.

- Modify an organization chart.

Lesson Introduction

Now that you've created and modified a flow chart, you're ready to apply your Visio skills to another popular diagram: the organization chart. If your business has more than one employee, you probably have a chart of the hierarchy, or will need to make one. Visio allows you to seamlessly create a professional organization chart, which can easily be modified as your organization evolves. In this lesson, you will build organization charts.

TOPIC A

Create an Organization Chart Manually

With the experience you've gained so far, you can conceive of the steps to create an organization chart: drag shapes for each individual onto the page, and align them in a vertical hierarchy using special connectors. Considering that organizations can have hundreds or even thousands of members, this could be a very time-consuming and repetitive task. Visio provides the tools to simplify your work, including a wizard and starter diagrams. In this topic, you will create an organization chart manually.

Organization Chart Elements

Organization Chart Elements

An *organization chart* allows you to depict the systematic flow of authority and responsibility within an organization. These charts can be used to depict superior-subordinate relationships, report hierarchies, and inter-department links in an organization.

In Visio, the **Organization Chart** template is organized differently from the previous templates you've encountered. A contextual tab, **Org Chart**, is added to the ribbon, housing the commands you will need to create the chart. This tab contains a gallery of **Shape** styles. Each style has its own stencil of organization chart shapes associated with it, and a default layout that is applied.

The **Org Chart** tab contains the following groups.

Group Name	Contains
Layout	Commands to choose the layout structure. Other commands fit the drawing to the page and create a synchronized copy.
Arrange	Commands for inserting illustrations, groupings, callouts, connectors, links, and text elements.
Shapes	A gallery of shape styles. Each style has its own stencil that is loaded into the Shapes window when that style is selected.
Picture	Commands for inserting photographs of personnel, and commands to manage these images in the diagram.
Organization Data	Commands to import or export organizational data and generate a report comparing data in two different versions of the chart.

Ask the students which Org Chart tab group will be most effective for them when working with organization charts.

Default Layout and Style

An organization chart always has a layout structure, which determines whether subordinates are displayed horizontally, vertically, or side by side.

The Multiple Shapes Master

When you create a new file, the default style is **Belt**, and the default stencil loaded into the Shapes window is **Belt–Organization Chart Shapes**. If you select a different Shape style from the **Org Chart** tab, the stencil associated with it will be loaded into the Shapes window, replacing the previous one.

The default setting is for the layout to automatically follow the **Shape** style selection, but this setting can be modified from the **Layout** menu in the **Layout** group.

Discuss with the students about the shape type they are most likely to select when using the **Add Multiple Shapes** dialog box.

The Multiple Shapes Master

The **Multiple Shapes Master** shape, in the **Organization Chart Shapes Stencil**, is one very important time-saving tool in Visio. This powerful shape has a built-in dialog box that allows you to specify the number of instances of a shape representing a position in the hierarchy. For example, if your organization is a call center with 40 support specialists at the same hierarchy level, they can be added to a diagram in one step.

The **Add Multiple Shapes** dialog box is displayed when you drag the **Multiple Shapes Master** onto the **Drawing** page. After the quantity, shape type, and position in organization are specified, the shapes are initially placed on the page in a selection box so they can be relocated before committing them to the drawing.

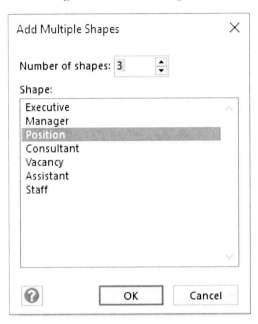

Figure 3-1: The Add Multiple Shapes dialog box with the shape and number of shapes selected.

 Access the Checklist tile on your CHOICE Course screen for reference information and job aids on How to Create an Organization Chart Manually.

ACTIVITY 3-1
Creating a New Organization Chart

Before You Begin
The Visio window is displayed. No file is open.

Scenario
B&B Fitness is planning to enlarge its operations this year and is expecting to add more personnel. Your manager has asked you to create a Visio diagram of the current organization to help in planning the expansion.

1. Open a new drawing.
   a) Select the **File** tab.
   b) In the **Backstage** view, select **CATEGORIES**.
   c) Select **Business→Organization Chart**.
   d) Verify that **US Units** is selected, and then select **Create**.

2. Set up the **View** options.
   a) On the **View** tab, in the **Show** group, verify that the **Ruler** check box is checked. Check the **Grid** check box.
   b) In the **Visual Aids** group, ensure that the **Dynamic Grid** and **Connection Points** check boxes are checked. Check the **AutoConnect** check box.

3. Place the Executive shape.
   a) Drag the **Executive Belt** shape from the stencil and place it so that the top-left corner is at (5, 8).
   b) Select the **Title** field, type *CEO*, select the **Name** field, and type *Seth Green*

    Note: If it is hard to get the text into the desired area on the shape, you may have to zoom in.

   c) Select outside the shape to finalize it.

4. Place subordinates by using the **Three positions** master.
   a) Select the **Three positions** shape and drag it over the Executive shape, so that the + portion of the pointer is on the center guideline of the CEO shape, and release it.
   b) Select outside the shape to finalize it.

   Verify that the three subordinates are spaced evenly under the CEO shape, with connectors in place.

Check if the students were able to get the Three positions shape exactly below the CEO shape. Also, ask them to ensure that they have enabled the AutoConnect feature and repeat the step. If they are not able to get the desired position shapes below the CEO shape, ask those students alone to position the + portion of the pointer on the downward facing Auto Connector arrow that appears when they select the CEO shape.

c) Label each shape, from left to right, as *Marketing Mgr., A. Brooks* , *Acct. Mgr., G. Pogal* , and *Training Mgr., D. Rogachev.*

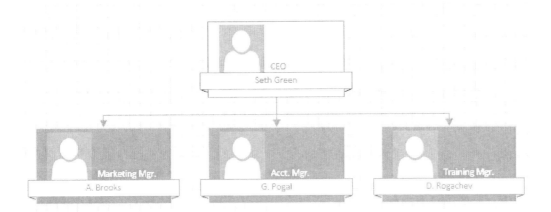

5. Place the assistant shape below the **Marketing Manager** shape and label the shape with the required name and title.

a) Drag the **Assistant Belt** shape and drop it over the **Marketing Manager** shape.

b) Select the title field, type *Marketing Asst.*, select the **Name** field, and type *R. Dado*

6. Use the **Multiple shapes** master to add staff shapes below the **Training Manager** shape.

a) Drag the **Multiple shapes** master, position it over the **Training Manager** shape, and release it.

b) In the **Add Multiple Shapes** dialog box, verify that the number of shapes is **3** and select **Staff** as the shape type.

c) Select **OK**.

d) Label the shapes with name and title, from upper to the lower: *Sam, Athletic Trainer, Joe, Athletic Trainer,* and *Dee, Personal Trainer.*

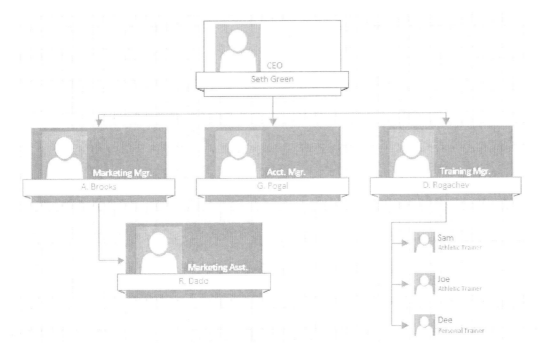

7. Save the drawing.

a) On the **Quick Access Toolbar**, select the **Save As** button.

b) Navigate to C:\091071Data\Building Organization Charts.

c) Save the file as *My B&B Org Chart.vsdx* and close it.

TOPIC B

Create Organization Charts by Using Starter Diagrams and the Organization Chart Wizard

Although creating an organization chart from a blank template enables you to customize the chart according to your organization's specifications, you might find that using sample layouts or a wizard to guide you in creating diagrams instantly to be helpful as well. Starter diagrams and the Organization Chart Wizard in Visio 2016 provide these options, which might make building an organization chart from scratch more straightforward.

The Organization Chart Wizard

The *Organization Chart Wizard* is a tool provided by Visio that automates the process of creating an organization chart.

You need to select the blank template from the Organization Chart Wizard home page to launch the Organization Chart Wizard. You can use the Organization Chart Wizard in one of two ways:

- Allow Visio to read personnel data from an external source such as an Excel file or a database.
- Specify information by using the wizard, which will create an Excel or delimited text file.

 Note: The first method listed, namely, allowing Visio to read personnel data from an external source, is an advanced topic that will be covered in Part 2 of this course.

Check with your students about how they plan to use the Organization Chart Wizard at their workplace.

Department Organization Chart

Department Organization Chart Starter Diagram

The *Department Organization Chart* is one of the built-in starter diagrams in the Organization Chart Wizard template in Visio 2016. This chart can be used to display the hierarchy levels along with the reporting relationships. It supports an attractive modern format that can be used to depict your organization structure effectively.

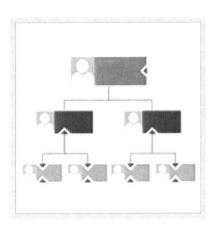

Department Organization Chart

Best used to show hierarchy levels and reporting relationships, in an attractive, modern format.
TIP: To show indirect reporting relationship, use the dotted line report shape.

○ Metric Units
● US Units

Create

Figure 3-2: The Department Organization Chart starter diagram as displayed on the Organization Chart Wizard template page.

Hierarchical Organization Chart Starter Diagram

Hierarchical
Organization Chart

The *Hierarchical Organization Chart* is the other built-in starter diagram in the Organization Chart Wizard template in Visio 2016. This chart allows you to display your organization levels along with the reporting relationships. You can depict the hierarchy levels by using the different shape sizes used in this template.

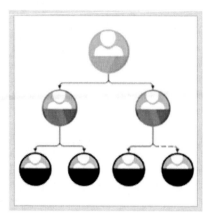

Hierarchical Organization Chart

Best used to show organizational levels and reporting relationships. Shape sizes help show hierarchy levels.

TIP: To add a new person, drop their shape onto their manager's shape, to instantly create the reporting relationship.

○ Metric Units
● US Units

Create

Figure 3-3: The Hierarchical Organization Chart starter diagram as displayed on the Organization Chart Wizard template page.

Access the Checklist tile on your CHOICE Course screen for reference information and job aids on How to Create Organization Charts by Using Starter Diagrams and Organization Chart Wizard.

ACTIVITY 3-2
Creating Organization Charts by Using Starter Diagrams

Before You Begin

The Visio window is displayed. No file is open.

Scenario

Your friend has requested you to help her create the organization chart for Fuller & Ackerman Publishing, a publishing firm. As you have limited time left for completing the task, you decide to use one of the starter diagrams to build the required department-wide chart.

You have been given the names of the personnel of the first three levels along with their designation.

These are listed in the table.

Designation	Reports To	Name
CEO	-	Dale Fuller
Marketing Manager	CEO	Greene Wood
Technical Manager	CEO	George Hill
Finance Manager	CEO	Suzy Sanders
Marketing Executive	Marketing Manager	Jim Smith
Marketing Executive	Marketing Manager	Vacant
Technical Consultant	Technical Manager	Michelle Frank
Finance Executive	Finance Manager	Jack Bill
Finance Assistant	Finance Manager	Trevor Bradley

Here is what the finished result should look like.

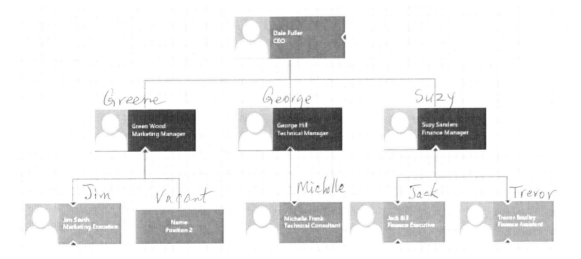

Note: As one marketing executive position is vacant, you can leave the corresponding box with the default name and position name in the organization chart. The color change will denote that the position is vacant.

1. Create the initial diagram layout by using the Department Organization Chart startup diagram.
   a) In the Visio window, select **File** and, in the right pane, select **CATEGORIES→ Business**. Then select the **Organization Chart Wizard** tile.
   b) Select **Department Organization Chart**, which is the second tile.
   c) Verify that **US Units** is selected and select **Create**.

2. Set the view options and remove the Tip pane.
   a) On the **View** tab, in the **Show** group, ensure that the **Grid** and **Ruler** check boxes are checked.
   b) View the contents of the **Tip** pane.
   c) Select the **Tip** pane and press **Delete** to remove the **Tip** pane from the drawing.

3. Include the CEO's name in the chart.
   a) For the **CEO** box, double-click the **Name** text box and type *Dale Fuller*

    Note: If it is hard to get the text into the desired area on the shape, you may have to zoom in.

   b) Select anywhere outside the **CEO** box to deselect it.

4. Update the chart to reflect the manager's name and designation for all three departments.
   a) On the **View** tab, in the **Visual Aids** group, check the **AutoConnect** check box.
   b) In the left pane, in the **Notch - Organization Chart Shapes** section, select **Manager Notch**.
   c) Drag it and place it on the **CEO** box.

d) Drag the newly inserted middle box and align it with the other two manager boxes and ensure that it lies exactly below the **CEO** tile.

 Note: If necessary, move the middle box suitably to ensure that only a single straight line connects it with the CEO box.

e) In the **Manager 1** box, double-click the **Name** text box and type *Greene Wood* as the manager's name.

f) In the **Manager 1** box, double-click the **Manager 1** text box and type *Marketing Manager* as the designation.

g) Repeat the previous two steps to fill up the names of the Technical Manager and the Finance Manager in the middle and the right titles, respectively, at the second level, as *George Hill* and *Suzy Sanders*.

5. Update the organization chart to include the Marketing Executive in the marketing department as given in the scenario.

a) Below the **Marketing Manager** box, in the **Position 1** box, double-click the **Name** text box and type *Jim Smith*

b) In the **Position 1** box, double-click the **Position 1** text box, and type *Marketing Executive* as the designation.

6. Update the organization chart to include a Vacant position in the marketing department.

a) Select the **Position 2** box, and select the **Org Chart** tab.

b) In the **Shapes** group, select **Change Position Type**.

c) In the **New position type** list, select **Vacancy** and select **OK**.
Verify that the Position 2 box's color changes to reflect the vacancy.

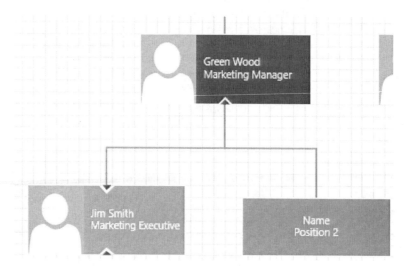

d) Select and move the Position 2 box 0.5 inch to the left.

7. Update the organization chart to include the Technical Consultant.
   a) In the left pane, in the **Notch - Organization Chart Shapes** section, select the **Consultant Notch**.
   b) Drag it and place it on the **Technical Manager** box.

    Note: Though the newly placed box overlaps the box on its right, ignore the error for now. You will address it shortly.

   c) In the newly placed box, double-click the **Name** text box and type *Michelle Frank*
   d) In the **Position 1** box, double-click the **Title** text box and type *Technical Consultant* as the designation.

   may jump around e) Drag the connector line between the **Technical Manager** and **Technical Consultant** shapes and move it below the **Technical Manager** box suitably to ensure that only a single straight line connects it with the **Technical Consultant** box.

    Note: You can also suitably resize the **Technical Manager** and **Technical Consultant** shapes to make the connector line straight.

The skill to resize the shapes and connectors is what needs to be practiced in this step. A perfect 100-percent match with the output is not needed, so ensure that students do not spend too much time on this step to make their drawing match the output.

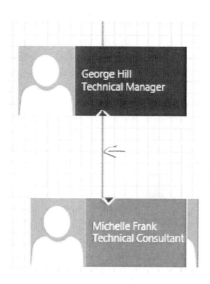

Use X in Size Position to move boxes otherwise lines change connections

8. Update the organization chart to include the names of the personnel of the finance department from the scenario.

   a) Select and move the Position 3 box 0.5 inch to the right to prevent it from overlapping with the consultant box.

   b) In the **Position 3** box, double-click the **Name** text box, and type *Jack Bill*

   c) In the **Position 3** box, double-click the **Title** text box and type *Finance Executive* as the designation.

   d) Repeat the previous two steps to fill up the name and designation for the Finance Assistant in the Position 4 box as *Trevor Bradley* and *Finance Assistant*, respectively.

   Check with the students and ask them to ensure that the Position 3 box does not overlap with Position 4 box on the right side.

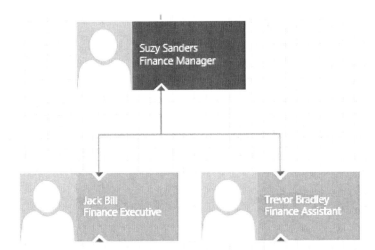

9. Save and close the file.

   a) On the **Quick Access Toolbar**, select the **Save As** button.

   b) Navigate to **C:\091071Data\Building Organization Charts**.

   c) In the **File name** field type *My Fuller Structure.vsdx* as the file name and select **Save**.

   d) Select **File** and, in the **Backstage** view, select **Close**.

ACTIVITY 3-3
Creating a Chart by Using the Organization Chart Wizard

Data File

C:\091071Data\Building Organization Charts\Employee Data.docx

Before You Begin

Navigate to **C:\091071Data\Building Organization Charts** and open the file **My B&B Org Chart.vsdx**.

Scenario

You will need to make organization charts for new branches of B&B Fitness that will be opening soon. You are wondering if it might be easier to create them by using the wizard. You decide to recreate the chart you created with the wizard to see if it is easier or less time consuming.

---

1. Launch the wizard and specify the file name and path for storing the import information specified by using the wizard.
   a) On the **Org Chart** tab, in the **Organization Data** group, select **Import**.
   b) In the **Organization Chart Wizard**, select the **Information that I enter using the wizard** option, and then select **Next.**
   c) On the next screen, select the **Excel** option.
   d) Leave the **New file name** field blank and select **Browse**.
   e) In the **Browse** screen, navigate to **C:\091071Data\Building Organization Charts**.
   f) For the name of the Excel file that will be created, type *mybb fit*, select a file type of **Microsoft Excel Workbooks**, and then select **Save**.

2. Specify the employee's data as the information that needs to be imported and save the spreadsheet file.
   a) When you are returned to the wizard with the new file name populated, select **Next**.
   b) Verify that a message appears that instructs you to type over the sample text, and select **OK**.
      Verify that an Excel file appears that contains fictitious names and data.
   c) Overwrite the Excel file with the following organizational data.

	Note: Ensure that you type only the values starting from the CEO row while leaving the second row blank and the heading row intact. Also, leave the **Telephone** field blank.

Name	Reports To	Title	Department	Telephone
Seth Green		CEO		
A. Brooks	Seth Green	Marketing Mgr.	Marketing	
G. Pogal	Seth Green	Acct. Mgr.	Accounting	
D. Rogachev	Seth Green	Training Mgr.	Training	

Name	Reports To	Title	Department	Telephone
R. Dado	A. Brooks	Marketing Asst.	Marketing	
Sam	D. Rogachev	Athletic Trainer	Training	
Joe	D. Rogachev	Athletic Trainer	Training	*Copy from above* *ctrl '*
Dee	D. Rogachev	Personal Trainer	Training	

> **Note:** You can either type the values from the above table manually or copy and paste the values from the data file, **Employee Data.docx**, which is available in the **C:\091071Data\Building Organization Charts** folder. You need to copy only the values starting from the CEO row and paste them below the blank second row in the Excel sheet.

   d) Select **Save** and then select the **Close** button to exit Excel. If necessary, close any open Microsoft Word windows.

3. Complete the remaining steps of the Organization Chart Wizard and compare the organization charts in the first and second pages of the file.

   a) If necessary, select the Visio window.

   b) On the next screen, verify that pictures will not be included. Select **Next**.

   c) On the next screen, verify that the wizard automatically breaks the chart across pages.

d) Select **Finish**.

Verify that the organizational chart has been created on page 2 of the file.

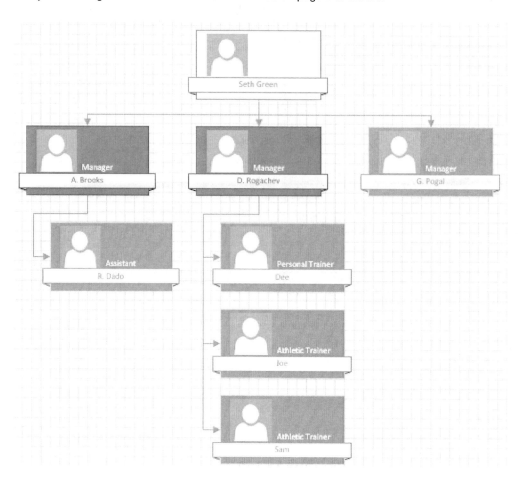

e) Compare the output of the wizard to the chart you made previously, on page 1. Verify that you were able to arrive quickly at a similar flowchart while performing fewer steps.

 Note: For more information, check out the LearnTO **Create a Family Tree** presentation from the **LearnTO** tile on the CHOICE Course screen.

You may want to show LearnTO **Create a Family Tree** from the CHOICE Course screen or have students navigate out to the Course screen and watch it themselves as a supplement to your instruction. If not, please remind students to visit the LearnTOs for this course on their CHOICE Course screen after class for supplemental information and additional resources.

TOPIC C

Modify an Organization Chart

As with any other Visio diagram, you may need to modify an organization chart, either due to your own refinements or based on stakeholder feedback. Visio supplies the tools to enhance the appearance of the chart. In this topic, you will modify an organization chart.

Formatting Tools

Visio's built-in organization chart formatting tools allow you to change the appearance of your diagram to meet the needs of your audience. For example, in a very large organization, you may want to hide subordinates to make the organizational structure fit into a single page. You may also want to change the spacing between shapes, change shape size, or add or remove informational fields that are displayed on each shape.

Report Connections

Report Connections is another useful feature that allows you to enhance your organization chart to show interactions between personnel on different teams. For example, when one subordinate trains a new staff member at the same level in the hierarchy, you can represent the same by using the Report Connections feature. Report connections are offered as shapes on the **Organization Chart** stencils.

 Access the Checklist tile on your CHOICE Course screen for reference information and job aids on How to Modify an Organization Chart.

ACTIVITY 3-4
Modifying an Organization Chart

Before You Begin

The file My B&B Org Chart.vsdx is open.

Scenario

You've just finished creating the organization chart, but there have already been some personnel changes. The accounting manager has been promoted to VP of finance, directly under the CEO, and will be supervising the marketing department. The marketing manager has resigned and the position is vacant. You need to update the organization chart to reflect these changes.

Here is what the finished result should look like.

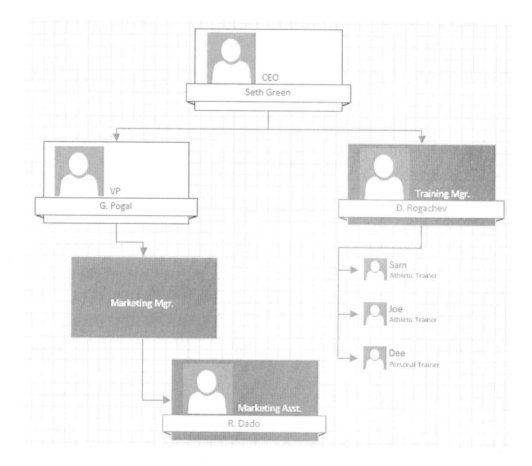

1. Change the position of the Acct. Mgr. G. Pogal to VP.
   a) Navigate to Page - 1 and select the shape labeled **G. Pogal**.
   b) On the **Org Chart** tab, in the **Shapes** group, select **Change Position Type**.
   c) In the **Change Position Type** dialog box, select the **Executive** position from the list.
   d) Select **OK**.

Note: Verify that the shape has changed to the executive style.

   e) Edit the title of G. Pogal to **VP**.

2. Rearrange the hierarchy so that the marketing department is now under the VP.
   a) On the **View** tab, in the **Visual Aids** group, uncheck the **Autoconnect** check box.
   b) Select the **Marketing Manager** shape, drag it over the VP, and drop it.

 Note: Verify that the diagram needs to be rearranged because the shapes are not arranged correctly.

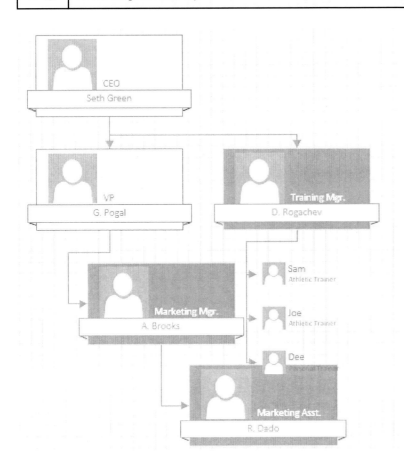

Use Org Chart Layout.
Choose *See Page 70*

Vacancy p 70

3. Fix the layout.

P.g 70

a) On the **Org Chart** tab, in the **Layout** group, select **Re-Layout**.

> **Note:** Verify that the connector between the **VP** and the **Marketing Manager** has an overly complicated path.

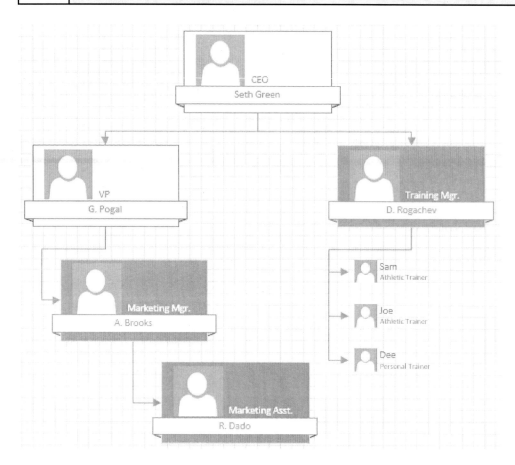

b) Move the connector ends so that there is a shape to shape connection between the **VP** and the **Marketing Manager**, which will make a neater path.

4. Change the position (shape) of the A. Brooks shape to Vacancy.

a) Right-click the **A. Brooks** shape.

b) Select the third option, **Change Position Type**, and select **Vacancy** from the list.

c) Select anywhere on the page to finalize the change.

Sometimes the existing text may appear to be uneditable when the position shape is changed to Vacancy. If this happens, just have the students undo the step and delete the text first, and then change the shape to Vacancy.

d) Delete the name from the shape, but retain the title.

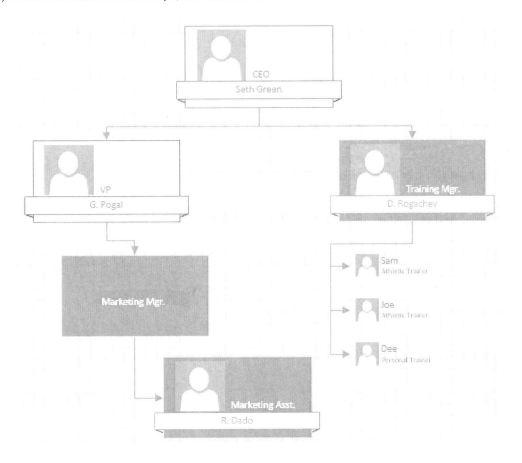

5. Save and close the file.

Summary

In this lesson, you represented an organization hierarchy as a Visio diagram by using the Organization Charts feature. Visio allows you to create organization charts in multiple ways: manually, by using the Organization Chart Wizard, or with starter diagrams. When you depict your organization chart in Visio, it will be clearly visible and you can make changes to it in the future easily. Further, you used the **Org Chart** tab commands to modify the diagram to reflect the changes in your organization and apply different styles to it.

Encourage students to use the social networking tools provided on the CHOICE Course screen to follow up with their peers after the course is completed for further discussion and resources to support continued learning.

Which Visio organization chart shapes would you use to represent your organization?

A: Answers will vary, but may include the Multiple Shapes Master that allows you to choose the type of position and the number of subordinates you want to add, or the Shape Options Field tab.

Will you build a chart manually, use the wizard, or use a starter diagram, and why?

A: Answers will vary, but may include using the wizard or starter diagram to save time, getting a pre-defined layout instead of having to build the diagram manually from scratch, or having to do only manual editing.

Note: Check your CHOICE Course screen for opportunities to interact with your classmates, peers, and the larger CHOICE online community about the topics covered in this course or other topics you are interested in. From the Course screen you can also access available resources for a more continuous learning experience.

4 | Designing a Floor Plan

Lesson Time: 40 minutes

Lesson Objectives

In this lesson, you will design a floor plan. You will:

- Use Visio to create a basic floor plan layout.

- Use Visio to model and test ideas such as zoom layouts.

Lesson Introduction

Modeling layouts in Visio can be easier than with paper layouts, especially when exact measurements are involved. And moving objects on the computer screen requires far less effort than moving real tables, chairs, and machinery around to find the perfect layout. Visio can serve as a capable modeling tool, enabling you to experiment with different layouts, share them with others, and revise them with minimal effort. In this lesson, you will design a floor plan.

TOPIC A

Make a Basic Floor Plan

You can use Visio's templates to depict the required layout in a diagram. Visio allows you to scale down the real-life objects to fit into a Visio drawing. With Visio's integrated measurement and scaling and intelligent objects, you can easily develop scaled diagrams such as floor plans, machine layouts, and so forth. In this topic, you will use Visio to create a basic floor plan layout.

Drawing Scale

Check with the students about the situations when they think the drawing scale of Visio will be useful at their workplace.

When you draw a floor plan on paper, you need to scale it down to fit the page size. In Visio, you can scale a large room to the size of a computer monitor screen or show a chair at the size of a coin. For example, if you draw a 3-foot-long coffee table at a size of 1 inch, its drawing scale will be 1:36 (1 inch:3 feet, or 1 inch:36 inches). In Visio, a default template shows the ruler's scale as it is printed. However, the floor plan template, like many other Visio templates, can conveniently show the scale as it would be in real life: the room in a floor plan is labeled in feet. The templates have predefined scales; however, you can set your own scale either for the whole drawing or for any page in the drawing. Conveniently, when a shape is dragged into the drawing, the shape resizes to match the scale setting.

Zero Point

The zero point of XY coordinates of the drawing is located in the bottom-left corner, but this can be changed if needed. For example, you may want to start measuring objects from the walls and not from the edges of the page. In this situation, you need to change the zero point to start from the walls instead of the page's edges.

Need for Creating Custom Room Shapes

Need for Creating Custom Room Shapes

Ask the students about how they think custom room shapes will be helpful in their projects.

The **Walls, Doors and Windows** stencil includes predefined room shapes: rectangular, L-shaped, and T-shaped. You can use these stencils directly for including these predefined room shapes in your floor plan. For making a floor plan for a differently shaped room, you need to create custom-shaped rooms by combining multiple space shapes. The space shapes can be found in the **Walls Shell and Structure** stencil. You can combine the space shapes by using the **Union** command. After you have obtained the required custom shape, you can convert the custom shape to a room and include it in your floor plan.

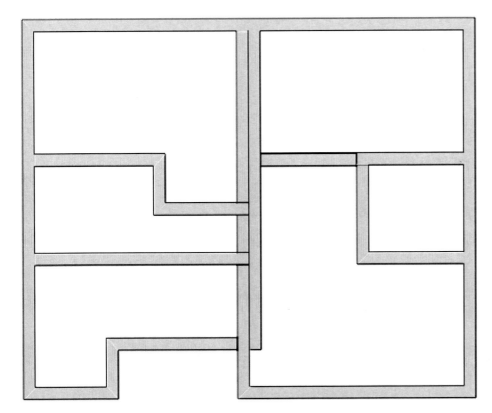

Figure 4-1: Custom wall shape created by combining multiple space shapes.

	Access the Checklist tile on your **CHOICE Course** screen for reference information and job aids on **How to Make a Basic Floor Plan.**

ACTIVITY 4-1
Making a Basic Floor Plan

Before You Begin
Visio window is displayed. No file is open.

Scenario
The marketing department at B&B Fitness has moved to another floor in the building and your department has received some extra space for expanding your offices. You want to convert an empty corner area to a small meeting room. The room will be laid out as shown. After you have the floor plan defined, you will experiment with furnishings to determine the best layout.

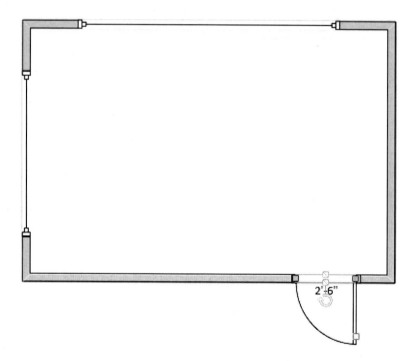

1. Start a new file by using the **Office Layout** template.
   a) Select the **File** tab.

b) In the **Backstage** view, select CATEGORIES→Maps and Floor Plans→Office Layout.

Office Layout

c) Verify that **US Units** is selected, and then select **Create**.

2. Add a room.
   a) Select the **Walls, Doors and Windows** stencil.
   b) Drag the rectangular **Room** shape from the stencil and align it at the center of the **Drawing** page.
   c) If needed, expand the Shapes window to make it wider by selecting the > sign next to the top-left corner of the **Drawing** page.

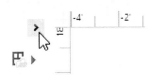

3. Make the room size 10 feet by 15 feet (10'×15'). *H   W*   Use Shape Data Palette
   Use Properties on next page

a) Right-click on a wall of the room and observe the options displayed in the drop-down menu.

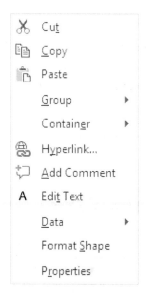

>
> **Caution:** If you observe a different drop-down menu, this means that you are in a text editing mode—that is, you missed the wall and clicked inside the room, causing Visio to switch to text-editing mode for the room shape. Just reselect, and be sure to observe the four-headed arrow as you select.

b) At the bottom of the menu, select **Properties**.

c) Type the numbers as shown below; verify that the units are filled in automatically and select **OK**.

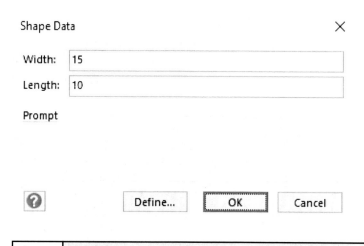

> **Note:** Don't worry that width is bigger than length.

4. Add the windows.

a) Drag windows to their locations as shown.

>
> **Note:** The windows snap in automatically to fit the wall orientation.

Properties 1 - 10ft
2 - 8ft

b) Size windows as shown.

>
> **Note:** Because you have already learned how to size shapes exactly, you can size them approximately in this activity, to save time.

5. Add a door.
   a) Drag a door to the location shown.
   b) Open the door to outside of the room by dragging the yellow handle on the door.

    Note: Alternatively, you can right-click the door and select **Reverse In/Out Opening.**

6. Save the drawing.
   a) On the **Quick Access Toolbar**, select the **Save As** button.
   b) Navigate to **C:\091071Data\Designing a Floor Plan**.
   c) Save the file as *My Fitness Floor Plan.vsdx*

TOPIC B

Model a Room Layout

Visio is more than just a drawing tool. You can use it to model and test ideas, such as meeting-room and factory-floor layouts, machine placement, and so forth. You can use the Visio diagram to determine the number of physical equipment pieces that can be placed in a room of the given dimension, or determine the change needed in the room size to accommodate a specific number of physical equipment pieces and machines. In this topic, you will use Visio to model and test ideas such as zoom layouts.

Visio as Modeling Tool

Visio shapes can be programmed with intelligent behavior that can save you significant effort when drawing charts and diagrams. For example, as you change dimensions of the conference room table shape, chairs are automatically added or removed based on the table dimensions. With an intelligent shape readjustment such as this, you can use the conference room table interactively to help determine the best layout.

Features such as intelligent shape readjustment are not merely a drawing convenience. They enable you to use Visio as a modeling tool. You can get an immediate sense of how many seats you can accommodate as you experiment with different table dimensions.

Objects such as windows and doors snap into position, and include features such as a functional door hinge that models the behavior of a real door. You can get a sense of where the door should be placed and which direction the door should swing.

 Access the Checklist tile on your CHOICE Course screen for reference information and job aids on How to Model a Room Layout.

ACTIVITY 4-2
Modeling a Room Layout

Before You Begin

Visio is open. You have created and saved a floor plan in **My Fitness Floor Plan.vsdx**.

Scenario

You have created the floor plan for your meeting room. You will now add a conference table and other items to the room, and you will experiment a bit with the layout to determine the best layout for up to five occupants.

Here is what the finished room layout should look like.

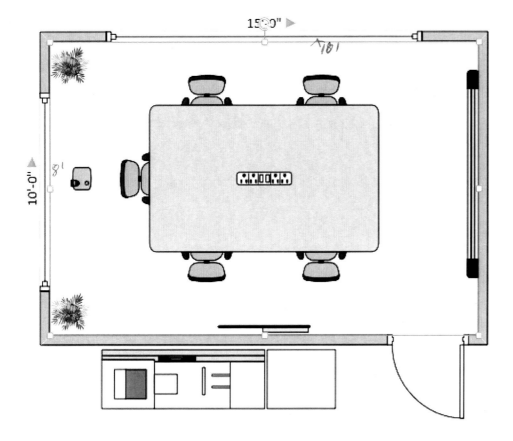

1. Add the table, plants, and a marker board.

    a) Select the **Office Furniture** stencil.

    b) Drag the **Multi-chair rectangle** table shape into the room.

    c) Turn the table sideways as shown by dragging a turning handle.

 Indicate to the students that the work is accomplished with less effort than in real life.

    d) Shorten the table by dragging its corner and verify that two extra chairs are removed.

    e) Select the **Office Accessories** stencil.

    f) Drag two **Palm plant** icons to the room and place them in the upper- and lower-left corners.

    g) Drag a **Marker board** to the bottom wall.

    h) Turn it sideways to align with the wall.

2. Add the computer projector and the screen.

    a) Select the **Office Equipment** stencil.

    b) Drag a **Projector** as shown.

    c) Add a **Projection screen** as shown.

 Note: You would need light tight blinds for using the projector; those will not be shown on the office plan but should be included in the accompanying documentation.

    d) In the **Shapes** window, select **SEARCH**. In the **Search shapes** text box, type *Duplicator* and select the **Start search** button to locate the **Duplicator** shape.

    e) Place the **Duplicator** shape outside of the meeting room as shown.

    f) Note that a person sitting by the screen would have trouble seeing it. Delete the chair that is near the projection screen as shown. You should get the result given in the scenario. Save the drawing.

3. Experiment with the layout.

    a) Change the size and position of layout elements to experiment with the following scenarios.

- Can you possibly fit a table with seven chairs in the room?
- What if the door has to swing into the room?
- If you can make the room wider (moving the right wall farther to the right), how wide would the room need to be to comfortably fit 11 chairs?

If you have some time to spare, ask the students to modify the floor plan for each of the situations listed below. Otherwise, ask the students to directly move to Step 4 after completing Step 2.

4. Save and close the drawing.

Summary

In this lesson, you learned how to make a basic floor plan in Visio and how to specify exact sizes for rooms and furniture. Visio has options that allow you to represent real-life objects on screen by using the drawing scale option to proportionally scale down objects compared to their actual size. As a modeling tool, Visio allows you to visualize the floor or plant layout on screen, and helps you to determine the number of pieces of machinery or equipment that can be accommodated within the given room size and the changes needed to accommodate the required number of pieces of equipment. After you make the necessary changes to the layout, you can implement it at the factory or office. In this way, you can potentially save time by avoiding any unnecessary rework.

In which projects would you make floor plans?

A: Answers will vary, but might include floor plans for home, office, and production facilities.

Where else could you use this workflow if not for floor plans? Think about projects outside of buildings or at a different size scale.

A: Answers will vary. Learners might say that they could use this workflow to map cubicle arrangements in an office, locations of electronic components on a card, landscaping design, sitting arrangements for a formal dinner, positions of players on the field in team games, and so on.

 Note: Check your CHOICE Course screen for opportunities to interact with your classmates, peers, and the larger CHOICE online community about the topics covered in this course or other topics you are interested in. From the Course screen you can also access available resources for a more continuous learning experience.

 Encourage students to use the social networking tools provided on the CHOICE Course screen to follow up with their peers after the course is completed for further discussion and resources to support continued learning.

5 | Building a Cross–Functional Flowchart

Lesson Time: 1 hour

Lesson Objectives

In this lesson, you will build a cross-functional flowchart. You will:

- Create a cross-functional flowchart.

- Apply styles to a cross-functional flowchart.

Lesson Introduction

In the previous lesson, you created simple flowcharts to represent a process. Even in these simple examples, the processes involved interactions between various departments in the organization. Now you will create a more sophisticated type of flowchart to map these interactions. In this lesson, you will build a cross-functional flowchart.

TOPIC A

Create a Cross-Functional Flowchart

When an organization wants to examine a process in more detail, one method is to map the flow of activity into and out of each department. The diagram that is used for this purpose is a cross-functional flowchart, also referred to as a swimlane chart. In this topic, you will create a cross-functional flowchart.

Cross-Functional Flowcharts

Cross-Functional Flowcharts

A *cross-functional flowchart* is a special type of flowchart that is used to illustrate a process flow involving multiple departments, companies, functions, or tasks, or the division of labor in an integrated process. Cross-functional flowcharts rely on a matrix structure to visually represent the involvement and communication between various units of an organization.

Vertical or horizontal bands, known as *swimlanes*, represent functional units, such as departments, teams, or even individuals. A complete process is mapped out from start to end, with each step placed in the band where it occurs.

This type of diagram is very useful in business analysis and planning to clarify the responsibilities of each unit in a process. These charts are useful in analyzing delays, as they will often bring out areas of duplication or extraneous processing.

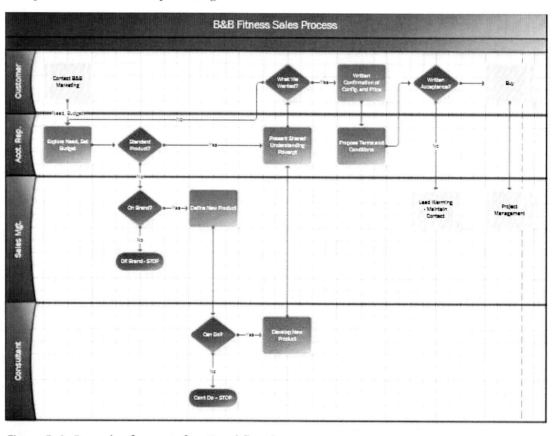

Figure 5-1: Example of a cross-functional flowchart.

Cross-Functional Flowchart Elements

The **Cross-Functional Flowchart** template provides two stencils, **Basic Flowchart Shapes** and **Cross-Functional Flowchart Shapes**, and adds the **CROSS-FUNCTIONAL FLOWCHART** tab to the ribbon. The **Cross-Functional Flowchart Shapes** stencil contains four special shapes, vertical swimlane and separator, and horizontal swimlane and separator. Separator shapes mark different phases of a process.

In addition to the blank template, the **Cross-Functional Flowchart** template in Visio 2016 contains three starter diagrams, **Horizontal Cross-Functional Flowchart**, **Shared Process Cross-Functional Flowchart**, and **Vertical Cross-Functional Flowchart**, which allow you to create flowcharts with different formatting and layouts.

The CROSS-FUNCTIONAL FLOWCHART Tab

The Cross-Functional Flowchart template and starter diagrams add a contextual tab named **CROSS-FUNCTIONAL FLOWCHART** to your Visio diagram. This tab contains three command groups, **Insert**, **Arrange**, and **Design**, that allow you to build your cross-functional flowchart. The table lists the functions of each of these command groups.

The CROSS-FUNCTIONAL FLOWCHART Tab

Command Group	Allows You To
Insert 	Add an additional swimlane or separator based on the current layout (horizontal or vertical), and add an additional page with a cross-functional flowchart based on the current layout.
Arrange 	Change the orientation of the swimlanes from horizontal to vertical, reverse the flow direction, and change margins within all swimlanes and phases.
Design	Rotate the line label, turn on and off display of title bar and separators, and change the visual style.

	Access the Checklist tile on your **CHOICE** Course screen for reference information and job aids on **How to Create a Cross-Functional Flowchart.**

ACTIVITY 5–1
Creating a Cross-Functional Flowchart

Before You Begin

The Visio window is displayed. No file is open.

Scenario

B&B Fitness markets a custom fitness plan to large corporations. A new sales kit was created and rolled out three months ago, but the results show that the plan needs improvement. There is too much variation in the length of the sales process, final product configuration, and customer expectations. You are assigned to work with the sales team to determine the root causes and propose a solution.

After talking with them, you realize that the sales tools are not being implemented at the proper times. Together with the team, you revise the process, implementing the sales tools based on observable and documentable customer behavior. You will use Visio to create a cross-functional diagram to document this process.

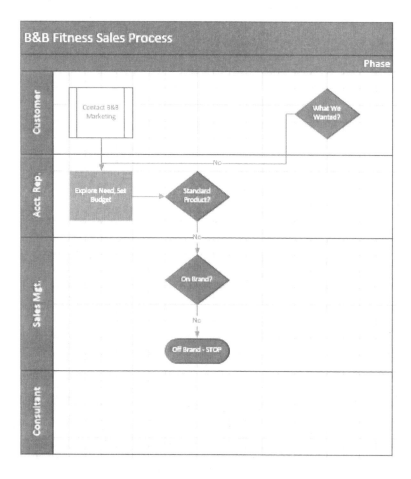

1. Create a new cross-functional flowchart by using the blank template.

   a) Select the **File** tab.

---

b) In the **Backstage** view, select CATEGORIES→Flowchart→Cross-Functional Flowchart.

 Note: Verify that the first tile, the blank template, is selected and **US units** is selected.

c) Select **Create**.

d) If necessary, when prompted for the default orientation, select **Horizontal** and select OK.

e) On the **View** tab, verify that the **Ruler** check box is checked and check the **Grid** check box.

2. Add two more horizontal bands to the chart.

a) In the Shapes window, select the **Cross-Functional Flowchart Shapes** stencil.

b) Drag the **Swimlane** master onto the **Drawing** page so its top edge aligns with the bottom edge of the second band.

c) When an orange highlight line appears along the joint edge, release the mouse button. Verify that the band is lengthened automatically to match the existing bands.

d) Select the **CROSS-FUNCTIONAL FLOWCHART** tab and then, in the **Insert** group, select **Swimlane** to add another horizontal band directly beneath the one you just created.

Swimlane Separator   Page

Insert

3. Label the bands (swimlanes) and the chart's title.

a) Double-click the title bar of the top Function lane and label it as *Customer*

b) Continue labeling the next three Function lanes, from top to bottom, as *Acct. Rep.*, *Sales Mgt.*, and *Consultant*

c) Select a blank area of the **Drawing** page under the last swimlane to exit the text mode.

d) Label the chart's title *B&B Fitness Sales Process*

4. Add a subprocess shape to the **Customer** swimlane.

a) In the Shapes window, select the **Basic Flowchart Shapes** stencil.

b) Drag the **Subprocess** master into the **Customer** band so that its top-left corner is at (1, 7.25).

c) Double-click the shape, type *Contact B&B Marketing*, and select outside the shape to exit text mode.

5. Add a process shape to the **Acct. Rep.** swimlane.

a) Move the pointer over the subprocess shape until the bottom **AutoConnect** arrow is highlighted.

b) In the **Quick Shapes** mini toolbar, select the **Process** shape, which is the first shape.

 Note: Verify that the shape is automatically placed in the **Acct. Rep** band.

c) Double-click the shape and type *Explore Need, Set Budget* and select outside the shape to exit text mode.

6. Add a decision shape to the **Acct. Rep.** swimlane.

a) Add a decision shape to the right of the process shape, dynamically connect to it, and label it as *Standard Product?*

7. Add a decision shape to the **Sales Mgt.** swimlane.

a) With the Connector tool selected, drag the **Decision** master and place it under the last decision shape, in the **Sales Mgt.** band, and label it as *On Brand?*

b) Double-click the connector between **Standard Product** and the **On Brand** shape and label it as *No*

8. Add a start/end shape to the **Sales Mgt.** swimlane.

a) Add a **Start/End** shape under the **On Brand** shape and label it as *Off Brand - STOP*

b) Label the connector between **On Brand** and **Off Brand - STOP** as *No*

9. Reposition a shape to the **Sales Mgt.** swimlane.

a) Enlarge the **Sales Mgt.** band by selecting its bottom edge and dragging it down until it lines up with the 3-inch line on the vertical ruler and contains the **Off Brand - STOP** shape.

 Note: You may need to move the **Off Brand - STOP** shape into the **Sales Mgt.** band.

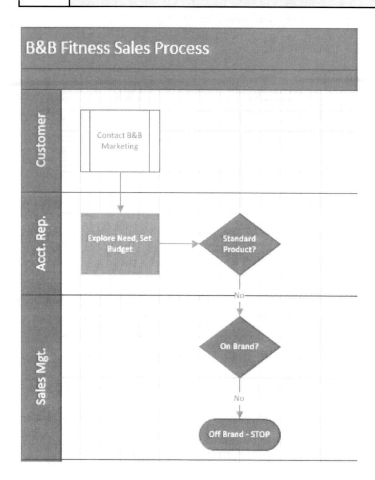

10. Add a decision shape in the Customer swimlane and connect it by using a connector.

a) In the **Customer** band, drag a decision shape and place it such that its center aligns with the horizontal ruler at the 5-inch mark.

b) Vertically align the new shape with the **Contact B&B Marketing** subprocess.

c) Label the new shape as *What We Wanted?*

d) By using the Connector tool under **Home→Tools**, add a glue-to-shape connector from the left side of **What We Wanted** to **Explore Need, Set Budget** and label it as *No*

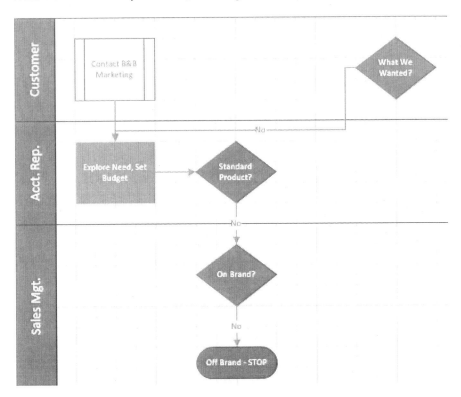

e) Under **Home→Tools**, select the **Pointer** tool.

f) Select the right edge of the phase and drag it to the 6-inch mark to resize the phase.

11. Save the diagram and keep the file open.

a) On the **Quick Access Toolbar**, select **Save As**.

b) Navigate to **C:\091071Data\Building a Cross-Functional Flowchart**.

c) In the **File name** text box, type *My B&B Sales Process* and verify that the type is **.vsdx**.

d) Select **Save**.

e) Leave the file open.

TOPIC B

Format a Cross-Functional Flowchart

You have created a cross-functional flowchart and populated it with content. You may find that you need to format it to make the information easier to read and to call attention to significant items. In this topic, you will apply styles to a cross-functional flowchart.

Cross-Functional Flowchart Formatting

The default formats for swimlanes may not always suit your needs. For example, you may need to change the orientation of lanes, spacing, or margins. In addition, similar to other Visio drawings, you may also apply other formats as well, such as color, fonts, and themes.

Styles

The style gallery in the **CROSS-FUNCTIONAL FLOWCHART** tab allows you to change the visual style of your cross-functional flowchart. You can apply fill and formatting effects to headings, swimlanes, and other elements of your cross-functional flowchart.

Visio provides twelve styles split into four groups, Style without fill and title, Style with fill but no title, Style with title but no fill, and Style with title and fill. Each of these groups contains three styles. Unlike other style galleries in Visio, this gallery does not show any *live preview* of the styles.

 Access the Checklist tile on your CHOICE Course screen for reference information and job aids on How to Format a Cross-Functional Flowchart.

ACTIVITY 5-2
Formatting a Cross-Functional Flowchart

Before You Begin
The file My B&B Sales Process.vsdx is open.

Scenario
Your sales process has been accepted by management and will be included in the sales kit. You decide to improve its appearance by cleaning up extraneous text, applying a more modern style, and centering the title. Also, you need to change the flowchart to a vertical orientation.

Here is what the modified cross-functional flowchart should look like.

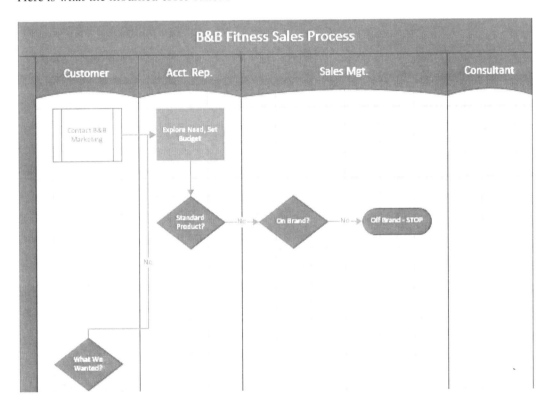

1. Remove the text **Phase** from the top bar.
   a) Double-click the text **Phase** and delete it.
   b) Select anywhere on the **Drawing** page.

2. Apply **Style No Fill 3** as the style for the flowchart.
   a) On the **CROSS-FUNCTIONAL FLOWCHART** tab, in the **Design** group, select **Style**.
   b) From the matrix of available styles, move the pointer over the third style in the top row and verify that the style is "Style No Fill 3" and select it.

   Verify that the swimlane names now have a decorative border.

3. Change the orientation of the flowchart to vertical and adjust a connector.

    a) Select **CROSS-FUNCTIONAL FLOWCHART**→**Arrange**→**Orientation**→**Vertical**.

       Verify that the flowchart changed to vertical orientation. Observe that the glue to shape connector between **What We Wanted** to **Explore Need, Set Budget** shape needs to be modified as it takes a longer path.

    b) Drag the connector to the left of the **What We Wanted** decision shape and move it to the top center of the decision shape.

       Verify that the connector path is now reduced.

4. Center the title.

    a) Select the **Home** tab.

    b) Double-click the chart title.

    c) In the **Paragraph** group, select the **Align Center** button (second row, second from left). Then deselect the title.

5. Save and close the file.

    a) On the **Quick Access Toolbar**, select **Save**.

    b) Close the file.

Summary

In this lesson, you represented a process in Visio by using a cross-functional flowchart and applied a style. Cross-functional flowchart or Swimlane chart allows organizations to map the flow of activity into and out of each department. This mapping, in turn, allows organizations to examine their processes in greater detail. Formatting a cross-functional flowchart allows you to make the information easy to read and call attention to significant items.

Can you think of a process in your organization that could benefit from being represented in a cross-functional flowchart?

A: Answers will vary, but may include hiring, purchasing, and new product development.

How can this kind of diagram help you to identify a process bottleneck?

A: Answers will vary, but may include visual identification of unnecessary paths between departments or extraneous approval steps.

Encourage students to use the social networking tools provided on the CHOICE Course screen to follow up with their peers after the course is completed for further discussion and resources to support continued learning.

Note: Check your CHOICE Course screen for opportunities to interact with your classmates, peers, and the larger CHOICE online community about the topics covered in this course or other topics you are interested in. From the Course screen you can also access available resources for a more continuous learning experience.

6 Designing a Network Diagram

Lesson Time: 45 minutes

Lesson Objectives

In this lesson, you will design a network diagram. You will:

- Create a network diagram.
- Use shape data.
- Use layers.

Lesson Introduction

Now that you've created both simple and more sophisticated flowcharts, you can progress to another type of diagram in which Visio excels: the network diagram. Visio is so popular for this application that network equipment manufacturers supply downloadable Visio network drawings on their websites. In this lesson, you will design a network diagram.

TOPIC A

Create Network Diagrams

A computer network diagram is a schematic depicting the nodes and connections in a computer network. It can also be used to depict, more generally, any telecommunications network. In this topic, you will create a network diagram.

Network Diagrams

Network Diagrams

Check with the students about the type of networks they are likely to use network diagrams to represent.

Network diagrams use symbols to represent common network devices such as servers and routers, and the style of lines between them indicate the type of connection. Clouds are used to represent networks outside the one of interest, without indicating their specifics.

Network diagrams can be made at different scales to show various levels of granularity. At the LAN level, individual nodes may represent individual physical devices, such as hubs or file servers, whereas at a higher level, nodes may represent networks. At higher levels, diagrams usually show representative devices, rather than the actual nodes. For example, if a network appliance is connected to many mobile devices, the diagram may show only one mobile device as a general representation.

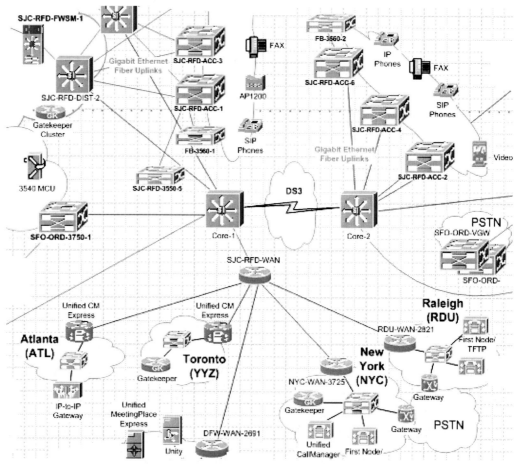

Figure 6–1: Visio Network Example: All test sites in North America Multisite Distributed deployment.

> **Note:** This network diagram is a fragment from **http://www.cisco.com/cisco/web/ docs/iam/unified/ipt611/Microsoft_Visio_Network_Topology_Diagrams.html**.

Template Categories and Starter Diagrams

The **Basic Network Diagram** and **Detailed Network Diagram** template categories contain two starter diagrams each in addition to the blank template. The starter diagrams provide built-in layouts that you can use to create your network diagrams. In addition, there are two 3-D categories that are related to the above two categories, but the 3-D categories do not contain any starter diagram.

The Intelligent Legend

Networking stencils contain an intelligent legend. When you drag a legend onto a drawing, it is automatically populated with the shapes used in the drawing and their quantities. If another type of shape is added, the legend will automatically be updated.

The Intelligent Legend

Symbol	Count	Description
	1	Switch
	1	Wireless access point
	1	Firewall
	1	Router
	1	Server
	1	Smart phone
	1	Hub
	3	PC
	1	Laptop

B&B Fitness Network

Figure 6-2: Legends of IT inventory in a network diagram.

Additional Network Shapes

Many of Visio's network diagram shapes are industry-standard topology shapes. As an industry standard for creating network diagrams, Visio has been used by IT professionals for over a decade. Many original equipment manufacturers (OEMs) have produced representations of their equipment in Visio stencils. One resource for accessing these stencils is the extensive collection at Visio Cafe (**www.visiocafe.com**), an independent non-profit website. The site hosts a collection of links to official IT industry Visio templates and stencils, composed of almost 5,000 shapes.

Ask the students about the types of stencils they are likely to download from **visiocafe.com** and the type of projects where they are likely to use such stencils.

Page Setup Dialog Box

The **Page Setup** dialog box allows you to control page size and printer settings. This dialog box contains five tabs, which are described in the table.

Page Setup Dialog Box

Tab	Description
Print Setup	Contains settings for the current printer. The Preview window shows the orientation of the current printer paper settings against the **Drawing** page.

Tab	Description
Page Size	Contains size and orientation settings for the **Drawing** page. You can define the page size for each page in a drawing. The Preview window shows the orientation of the paper against the **Drawing** page.
Drawing Scale	Substitutes one measuring system for another. For example, in a small drawing, 1 inch may represent 1 foot at the actual size. This is helpful for floor plans and other architectural drawings.
Page Properties	Allows you to specify a name for the page, set the desired measurement units, and assign a background page. Background pages can be used to add common page elements such as page numbers and borders across multiple pages.
Layout and Routing	Allows you to define how shapes and lines will appear when they get close to each other or cross.

Page Break

Page breaks, when displayed, can help you arrange items in a drawing. With page breaks, you can avoid placing objects or fields too close to margins. Page breaks are determined by the page's print margins.

 Access the Checklist tile on your CHOICE Course screen for reference information and job aids on How to Create a Network Diagram.

ACTIVITY 6-1
Creating a Network Diagram

Do this exercise again.

Before You Begin
The Visio window is displayed. No file is open.

Scenario
B&B Fitness' annual inventory is scheduled for next week, and your coworker has been assigned the task of surveying the current IT equipment. You offer to help your coworker make a Visio network diagram so the equipment and connections can be documented more easily.

Here is what the finished diagram should look like.

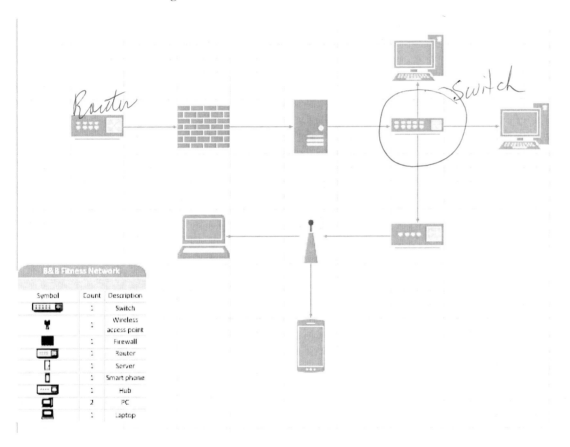

Symbol	Count	Description
	:	Switch
	:	Wireless access point
	:	Firewall
	:	Router
	:	Server
	:	Smart phone
	:	Hub
	2	PC
	:	Laptop

B&B Fitness Network

1. Create a blank network diagram and verify its view settings.
   a) In the Visio window, select the **File** tab.
   b) Select **CATEGORIES→Network→Basic Network Diagram**.
      Verify that the blank template is selected.
   c) Verify that **US units** is selected and select **Create**.
   d) Select the **View** tab and in the **Show** group, ensure that the **Ruler** check box is checked, and check the **Grid** check box.

e) In the **Visual Aids** group, ensure that the **Dynamic Grid** check box is checked, and check the **AutoConnect** check box.

2. Change the page settings so that all connections will be straight lines.
   a) In the Shapes window, verify that the **Network and Peripherals** stencil is active.
   b) In the lower part of the drawing, above the status bar, right-click the tab labeled **Page-1** to bring up a menu.
   c) Select **Page Setup→Layout and Routing**.
   d) From the **Style** drop-down list, select **Center to Center**.
   e) If necessary, from the **Appearance** drop-down list, select **Straight**.
   f) Select **OK**.

3. Add **Router**, **Firewall**, **Server**, and **Switch** shapes to the drawing.
   a) Drag the **Router** shape from the stencil to the page and drop the left corner of the selection box close to the X, Y position (1,7). Zoom in, if needed.
   b) Drag the **Firewall** shape from the stencil over the **Router** shape until the right **AutoConnect** arrow is highlighted and then drop it.
   c) Drag the **Server** shape from the stencil over the **Firewall** shape until the right **AutoConnect** arrow is highlighted and drop it.
   d) Drag the **Switch** shape from the stencil over the **Server** shape until the right **AutoConnect** arrow is highlighted and drop it.

4. Add a **Hub**, a **Wireless Access Point**, and a **Smartphone**.
   a) Drag the **Hub** shape from the stencil over the **Switch** shape until the bottom **AutoConnect** arrow is highlighted and drop it.
   b) Drag the **Wireless Access Point** shape from the stencil over the **Hub** shape until the left **AutoConnect** arrow is highlighted and drop it.
   c) Drag the **Smartphone** shape from the stencil over the **Wireless Access Point** shape until the bottom **AutoConnect** arrow is highlighted and drop it.

5. Add a **Legend** shape.
   a) Drag the **Legend** shape from the stencil and drop it near (0,5.5).
      Verify that the legend includes all the shapes used in the drawing and their quantities.
   b) Widen the legend to expand the description by pulling the middle selection handle on the right side.
   c) Double-click the **Legend** title and type *B&B Fitness Network*. Then double-click the subtitle and press the **Spacebar** to remove all text from there.

Rt click Edit Text

6. Add two **PCs** to the switch.
   a) Activate the **Computers and Monitors** stencil by selecting its title bar.
   b) Move the pointer over the **Switch** toward the top **AutoConnect** arrow, select the **PC** shape (the first shape) on the **Quick Shapes** mini toolbar, and release it.
      Observe that a horizontal dotted line, which represents a page break, appears and the PC is placed in a different page compared to the other objects and will need to be manually moved to be in the same page as other objects of the drawing. Verify that a **PC** is added to the legend.
   c) Reposition the **PC** to be located at (7,8) to keep it within the page.
   d) Move the pointer over the switch toward the right **AutoConnect** arrow, select the **PC** shape on the **Quick Shapes** mini toolbar, and release it.

Switch on right

7. Add a **Laptop** shape to the wireless access point.
   a) Drag the **Laptop** shape from the stencil over the **Wireless Access Point** shape, move toward the left **AutoConnect** arrow, and release it.
      Verify that a laptop is added to the legend.

8. Save the file.
   a) On the **Quick Access Toolbar**, select **Save As**.
   b) Navigate to C:\091071Data\Designing a Network Diagram.

c) In the **File name** text box, type *My Network*, select **.vsdx** as the file type, and select **Save**. Leave the file open.

TOPIC B

Use Shape Data

You've created a basic network diagram, but because it will also serve as an inventory tool, you want to add more information to it. Visio provides the Shape Data feature, which you can use to add conceptual depth to a diagram by letting the shapes serve as information warehouses. In this topic, you will use shape data.

Shape Data

Shape Data

Discuss with students the types of shapes and projects for which they think Shape Data fields will be useful.

Shape data is a set of contextually relevant fields that are a built-in property of a shape. For example, the **Shape Data** fields for a firewall include **Asset Number**, **Serial Number**, **Location**, and **Manufacturer**.

The fields for a consultant shape in an organization chart include **Department**, **Telephone**, **Name**, and **Email**. By default, shape data is not displayed in the drawing, but you can display and modify it by using a dedicated task pane.

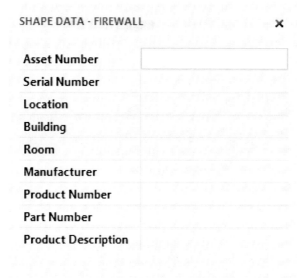

Figure 6-3: Shape Data fields of a Firewall shape.

> **Access the Checklist tile on your CHOICE Course screen for reference information and job aids on How to Use Shape Data.**

ACTIVITY 6-2
Using Shape Data

Data File

C:\091071Data\Designing a Network Diagram\Shapes Data.xlsx

Before You Begin

The file My Network.vsdx is open in Visio.

Scenario

You decide to use shape data in the network diagram so that it can be used by the inventory team. You decide to add the asset number, serial number, and room number.

1. Because all of these network items are in the same building, select all of them and specify the building name as **Main**.
   a) Select **View→Show→Task Panes** to display the **Shape Data** task pane.
   b) If necessary, drag the **Shape Data** task pane to the right of the drawing so it doesn't obscure the drawing page.
   c) Select all shapes by pressing **Ctrl + A**; then, in the **Shape Data** pane, select the **Building** field and type *Main*
   d) Select anywhere on the **Drawing** page to clear the shape selection.

      Verify that the **Shape Data** was specified by selecting a PC and observing the **Shape Data** for the building.

2. Select the **Router**, **Firewall**, and **Server** shapes and specify *300* as the room number.
   a) Select the **Router** shape, hold down the **Shift** key, and select the **Firewall** and **Server** shapes.
   b) In the **Shapes Data** pane, select the **Room** field and type *300*

3. Select the **Upper PC** and the **Middle PC** shapes and specify *310* as the room number.
   a) Select the **Upper PC** shape, hold down the **Ctrl** key, and select the **Middle PC** shape.
   b) In the **Shapes Data** pane, select the **Room** field and type *310*

4. Select the remaining shapes individually, select the appropriate fields, and specify the information given in the following table.

Shape	Asset #:	Serial #:	Room:
Router	145	115	300
Firewall	146	116	300
Server	147	117	300
Switch	148	119	301
Upper PC	150	211	310
Middle PC	151	212	310
Hub	153	214	320

To save time, you can instruct the students to specify only the shape data for the first four items. Point out that the room numbers 300 and 310 are displayed for the individual shapes in those rooms because multiple objects were selected when specifying the room numbers. Also, students can copy and paste values from the data file **Shapes Data.xlsx**.

Shape	Asset #:	Serial #:	Room:
Wireless Access Point	154	215	
Smartphone	155	216	
Laptop	156	217	

5. Close the **Shape Data** pane and save the file.

TOPIC C

Use Layers

Visio allows you to assign shapes to a layer and assign common properties to all shapes in that layer. For example, when creating a complex network diagram for a system with hundreds of components, you may want to assign all the higher-level components, such as servers, to one layer, and the desktops to another. You can then set the properties for each layer in one easy command. For example, you can turn the visibility of desktops off to simplify the diagram. In this topic, you will use layers.

Layers

Layers are like clear drawing sheets placed on top of one another, merging to produce a finished drawing. Layers provide additional control over elements in a drawing; for example, you can control which elements of a drawing to view or print. You can also use layers to group related types of shapes. When working with drawings that contain many shapes and connectors, you can use layers to group the elements by type. This allows you to selectively view each shape type and work on them individually.

Layers

Ask the students to list the benefits of layers and how they plan to use them in their future projects.

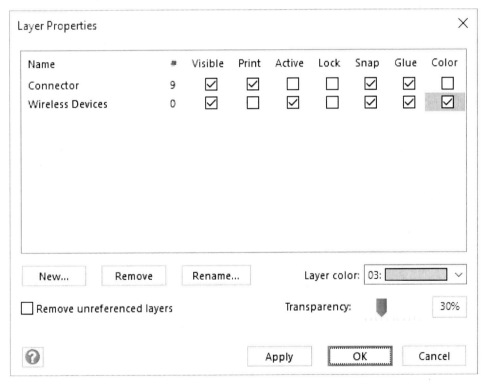

Figure 6-4: The properties of a new layer named Wireless Devices.

When you use certain templates, some types of shapes are assigned automatically to default layers when you drag them to the drawing page. For example, in a workflow or network diagram, connectors are assigned automatically to the **Connector** layer. You can view the default layer assignment by selecting an item and viewing the **Layer Properties** dialog box. This dialog box allows you to create a new layer and specify the various properties of the layer, such as **Visible**, **Print**, **Active**, **Lock**, and **Color**.

 Access the Checklist tile on your **CHOICE** Course screen for reference information and job aids on **How to Use Layers**.

ACTIVITY 6-3
Using Layers

Before You Begin
The file My Network.vsdx is open in Visio.

Scenario
The network diagram that you made for the inventory was well received, and your manager wants to use it to plan the network of the proposed expansion. You decide that it would be best to put all of the wireless devices on a separate layer to make it easier to view.

1. Adjust the View settings to prevent new connections from being added inadvertently while selecting.
   a) In the Visio window, on the **View** tab, uncheck the **AutoConnect** check box.

2. Create a layer to use for wireless devices and set its properties.
   a) Select the laptop shape on the drawing.
   b) On the **Home** tab, in the **Editing** group, select **Layers→Layer Properties**.
   c) In the **Layer Properties** dialog box, select the **New** button.

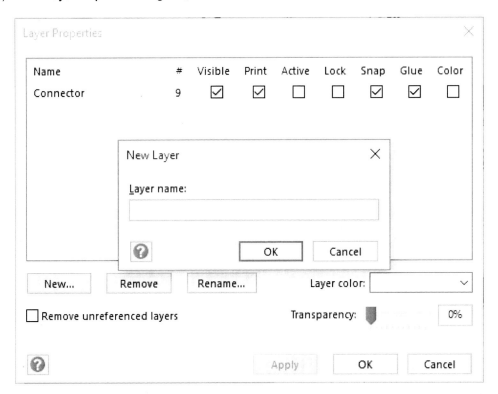

   d) Type *Wireless Devices* and select **OK**.
   e) Uncheck the **Print** check box.
   f) Check the **Active** check box so that any new shapes on the drawing will automatically be created on this level.
   g) Check the **Color** check box.

h) Set the layer color to lime green (**03**) and the transparency to **30%**. Select **OK**.

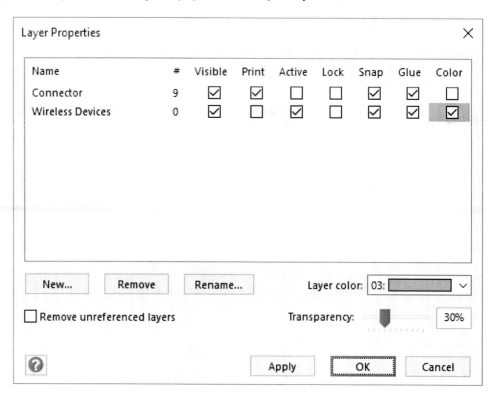

3. Assign the wireless devices to the layer **Wireless Devices**.
   a) On the **Drawing** page, select the laptop, press and hold the **Shift** key, and select the smartphone shapes and their connectors to the wireless access device.
   b) On the **Home** tab, in the **Editing** group, select **Layers→Assign to Layer**.

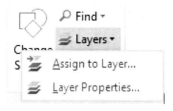

   c) In the dialog box, check the **Wireless Devices** layer name check box.
   d) If necessary, uncheck the **Connector** check box.
   e) Select **OK**.
   f) Select anywhere on the drawing but not on a shape.
      Verify that the selected shapes and connectors appear in green on the drawing.

4. Add another shape to the drawing.
   a) Drag another **Laptop** onto the drawing and release it to the right of the **Smartphone** shape.
      Verify that the shape appears in green.

    Note: There is no need to connect this laptop, as it is only demonstrating that any new shapes that are added will be created on the Wireless Devices level.

5. Turn off the visibility of the Wireless Devices level.
   a) On the **Home** tab, in the **Editing** group, select **Layers→Layer Properties**.
   b) For the **Wireless Devices** layer, uncheck the **Visible** check box.

   c) Select **OK**.

      Verify that the devices on the **Wireless Devices** layer no longer appear in the diagram.

 Note: You can easily display them again by checking the **Visible** check box in the **Layer Properties** dialog box.

6. Save the diagram and close it.

Summary

In this lesson, you represented a network in Visio, and modified it by adding shape data and layers. A network diagram allows you to represent the nodes and connections in any computer network, or generically, any telecommunications network. You can use the Shapes Data feature to add more information about the shapes in your network diagram. Further, layers allow you to add similar shapes to a group and assign common properties to all the shapes in the layer.

Encourage students to use the social networking tools provided on the CHOICE Course screen to follow up with their peers after the course is completed for further discussion and resources to support continued learning.

Which network diagram feature would be most helpful to you in mapping your network?

A: Answers will vary, but may include the variety of stencils and shapes available, context sensitive legend, shape data, and the layer feature.

Can you think of any other kinds of diagrams you will make with Visio that can take advantage of shape data?

A: Answers will vary, but may include organization charts, floor plans, and work flows.

> **Note:** Check your CHOICE Course screen for opportunities to interact with your classmates, peers, and the larger CHOICE online community about the topics covered in this course or other topics you are interested in. From the Course screen you can also access available resources for a more continuous learning experience.

7 | Styling a Diagram

Lesson Time: 30 minutes

Lesson Objectives

In this lesson, you will style a diagram. You will:

- Identify and use shape and connector style commands.

- Identify and use themes and variants.

- Add a container.

Lesson Introduction

You've concentrated on the content of your diagrams and know how to create flowcharts, cross-functional flowcharts, organizational charts, floor plans, and network diagrams in Visio. To give your work a professional appearance and to conform to the branding choices of your organization, you also need to consider the visual style. This lesson will introduce Visio's design options, which are covered in greater detail in the next course in the series. In this lesson, you will style a diagram.

TOPIC A

Modify Shape and Connector Styles

Up until this point, you have used the default versions of Visio's shapes and connectors. However, shapes and connectors have many properties that can be modified to alter their appearance. In this topic, you will identify and use shape and connector style commands.

Visio Design Tools

Visio Design Tools

Ask the students about the design tools they are likely to use often at work and why they would use them.

Visio provides a variety of tools to craft the visual style of your diagram. Line width and shape fill can be modified, connector paths can be varied, and color-coordinated themes and variants can be applied to the entire diagram.

Here are some of the properties that can be modified for lines and shapes from the **Home** tab, **Shape Styles** group. If an element is selected on the drawing, a live preview will be displayed as you point to these options.

Element	Function
Fill→Color	Fills the inner area of a selected shape with color, either solid or varied in a pattern or gradient. The colors that are available are derived from the currently selected design theme, in addition to standard colors.
Line→Color	Controls the color of the selected line. These can be applied to connectors or to the lines that comprise a shape. The colors that are available are derived from the currently selected design theme, in addition to standard colors.
Line→Weight	Contains options for different line thicknesses. These can be applied to connectors or to the lines that comprise a shape.
Line→Dashes	Contains options for various dash intervals and dot-and-dash combinations.
Line→Arrows	Contains options for the end shapes of a selected connector, ranging from three different arrow shapes to round caps.

Advanced commands for modifying fill and line properties can be accessed by selecting the dialog box launcher in the lower-right corner of the **Shape Styles** group. Effects such as shadows, reflection, glow, soft edges, bevel, and 3-D rotation can be accessed from the **Effects** command.

Connector Path Styles

There are also stylistic considerations with regard to connector paths. The three styles available are **Right Angle**, **Straight Lines**, and **Curved Lines**. These can be modified for selected connectors, or the default for the entire diagram can be set.

 Note: The elements of the Visio drawing interface may appear differently depending on whether the screen is fully maximized.

 Access the Checklist tile on your CHOICE Course screen for reference information and job aids on How to Modify a Connector.

ACTIVITY 7-1
Modifying Chart Visual Styles and Connector Styles

Data File

C:\091071Data\Styling a Diagram\Organization Chart.vsdx

Before You Begin

The Visio window is displayed. No file is open.

Scenario

You are in charge of building a team for a fitness consultation project. The client is a design firm startup and you want to include a visually appealing diagram of your team's hierarchy in a presentation to the client. You have an organization chart that you created that shows the structure of the team, and now you want to give it more modern styling. You decide to try different Org Chart themes and connector styles.

1. Try different organization chart visual styles.

   a) Navigate to the **C:\091071Data\Styling a Diagram** folder, and select the file **Organization Chart.vsdx** to open it.

   b) Select **Org Chart→Shapes** and from the list of shape styles, select the shape styles such as **Coin**, **Panel**, **Petals**, and **Stone** in sequence.

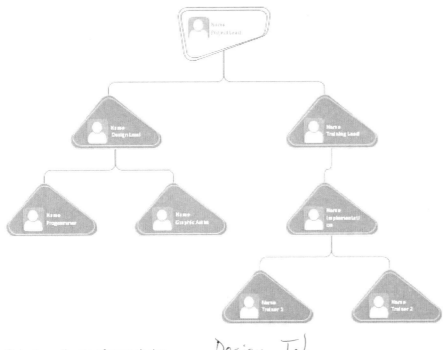

   c) Select any theme of your choice.   *Design Tab*

2. Try different connector styles.

   a) From **Design→Layout**, from the **Connectors** menu, select **Straight Lines** and observe the result.

        b) Select **Curved Lines** and observe the result.

3. Save the file.

        a) On the **Quick Access Toolbar**, select **Save As**.

        b) Navigate to **C:\091071Data\Styling a Diagram**.

        c) In the **File Name** text box, type *My Organization Chart*, select the **.vsdx** file type, select **Save**, and close the file.

TOPIC B

Apply Themes and Variants

Visio supplies a set of color themes and variants to simplify the job of giving your diagram a professional look. The style choices range from solid professional to contemporary and stylish. Each of the themes comes with four variants that provide distinctive color schemes and shapes while remaining within the aesthetic concept of the theme. In this topic, you will identify and use themes and variants.

Design Themes and Variants

Themes are predefined sets of colors and styles that you can quickly apply to a drawing. Themes control more than color applied to the shapes—they also set the fonts and effects used, according to combinations developed by graphics professionals. Individual shapes can be formatted further by using Quick Styles, which are based on the selected theme and its variants.

Design Themes and Variants

In addition to the design themes, Visio 2016 contains three Office themes for the entire Visio environment, namely, **Colorful**, **Dark Gray**, and **White**. The default theme is **Colorful**. In Visio, this theme displays the title bar, ribbon tabs, and **Backstage** view in the default dark blue color. The **Dark Gray** theme presents the interface with high contrast by applying the dark gray color throughout the interface except the currently displayed page and the thumbnails of shapes from the currently selected stencil in the Shapes window. The **White** theme presents a clean look by applying white color to the interface components.

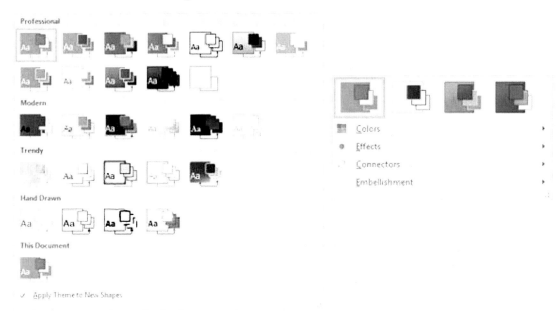

Figure 7-1: The design themes and variants that can be applied to a Visio drawing.

 | Access the Checklist tile on your CHOICE Course screen for reference information and job aids on **How to Use Themes, Variants, and Quick Styles.**

ACTIVITY 7-2
Applying Themes to a Diagram

Data File

C:\091071Data\Styling a Diagram\B&B Fitness Inventory.vsdx

Scenario

Your coworker has created a cross-functional flowchart for an upcoming inventory. She based the diagram on a Visio 2010 sample template for an audit process that she downloaded from the Visio website (**http://visio.microsoft.com/en-us/download/confirmation.aspx?id=26516**), and adapted the content for the inventory. She is happy with the content, but doesn't think the diagram has the right "look." You agree to help her modify the diagram to "look and feel" like a B&B Fitness document.

---

1. Open the file **B&B Fitness Inventory.vsdx** and apply the **Office** theme.
   a) In the Visio window, from the **Backstage** view, navigate to the **C:\091071Data\Styling a Diagram** folder.
   b) Select the file **B&B Fitness Inventory.vsdx** and open it.
   c) From **Design→Themes**, scroll up in the list and select the first theme, **Office**.

2. Modify the color of the text in the **Reporting** swimlane so it will be easier to read.
   a) Select the header of the **Reporting** swimlane.

      Verify that the entire column is selected and is outlined in gray.
   b) Select the header again so that it is highlighted with the selection handles displayed, then hold **Shift** and select the two shapes below it so that all three are selected.

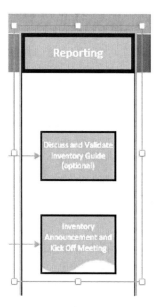

   c) From **Home→Shapes Styles**, select **Fill**.
   d) In the color display, under **Theme Colors**, find the current fill color, **Gold Accent 4**, which is highlighted in red.

e) Find the fourth color underneath it, **Gold Accent 4, Darker 25%**, and select it.

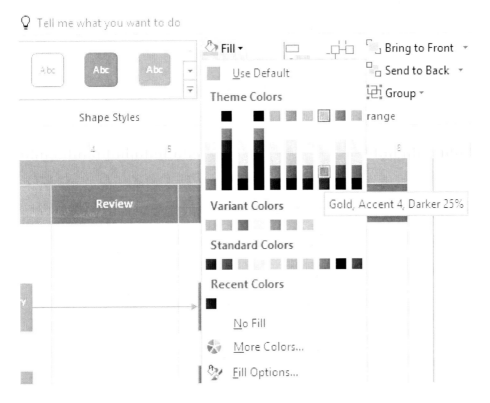

f) Select anywhere outside the swimlane to finalize the change.

Verify that the fill color is now darker and it is now easier to read the text.

3. Shift text vertically in two decision shapes so it fits onto the shapes.

a) In the **Planning** band, select the text in the decision shape labeled **Approve Inventory Guide**.

b) Select **Home→Paragraph→Align Top**.

c) In the **Review** band, select the text in the decision shape **Review Inv. Report & Sign Issuance Clearance**.

d) Select **Home→Paragraph→Align Bottom**.

4. Save the diagram in the directory **C:\091071Data\Styling a Diagram** as *My B&B Fitness Inventory dsgn.vsdx*. Leave the diagram open.

TOPIC C

Use Containers

As a diagram gets more complex, you may want to visually group shapes to improve the organization and clarity of your work. Visio meets this need by supplying containers, which are labeled boxes that you can create around selected shapes. In this topic, you will add a container.

Containers

A *container* is a special type of object that allows you to organize and define logical groupings when working with complex drawings in Visio. When you move a container, the shapes contained within it move as well. If you add a container with nothing selected, the container is inserted at the center of the drawing. You can add text to, resize, and reposition the container as needed. Because the container doesn't have a relationship with any shapes, moving it will not affect any other shapes on the drawing.

Containers

Ask the students about the type of Visio projects in which they may want to use containers at their workplace.

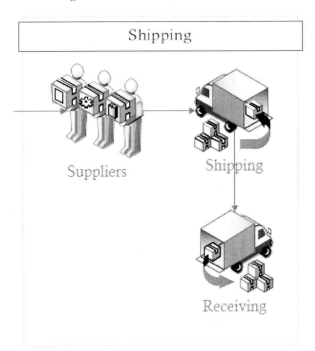

Figure 7–2: A sample container included in a drawing.

Lists

A *list* is a special type of container available in only some specific Visio templates. Lists automatically sequence the items that are placed within them. Examples of list containers include Swimlane shapes in the **Cross-Functional Flowchart** template and control shapes such as the list box in the **Wireframe** template. In addition, the legend shapes added to data graphics also have the characteristics of a list. Each of the list items can be resequenced by manually rearranging the items within the list.

Lists

Swimlane shape added to cross-functional flowchart

List box item added to List box control in Wireframe template

Figure 7-3: Examples of list containers.

Container Customization

If you move, copy, or delete a container, its contents will also be affected. However, the shapes inside the container are not in a group, so you can modify individual members directly without needing to ungroup and regroup.

The text properties of the header can be modified by using the **Home** tab's **Font** and **Paragraph** group commands. When you select a container, a contextual tab is added to the ribbon that provides important customization commands, such as container body and heading styles. The contextual tab allows you to lock and disband a container.

Lock and Disband a Container

You can lock a container to ensure that no new shapes are added to or deleted from the container. However, you can still move objects within a locked container.

When you disband a container, it will be removed but the shapes in the container will remain.

> Access the Checklist tile on your **CHOICE** Course screen for reference information and job aids on **How to Manage Containers**.

ACTIVITY 7-3
Adding a Container

Before You Begin
The file My B&B Fitness Inventory dsgn.vsdx is open.

Scenario
Your drawing is almost finished, but you want to add a few more finishing touches. You decide to add a container to enclose the steps related to the draft inventory document, to help clarify the diagram. You also want to improve the title of the diagram.

1. Add a container to highlight the steps relating to the draft inventory.

    a) In the Visio window, select all the shapes and connectors that are related to the draft by using an area select.

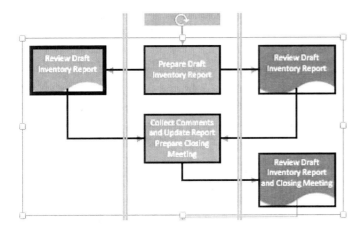

    b) From **Insert→Diagram Parts**, select **Container**.
    c) Select the **Translucent** style, the second from the left on the bottom row.

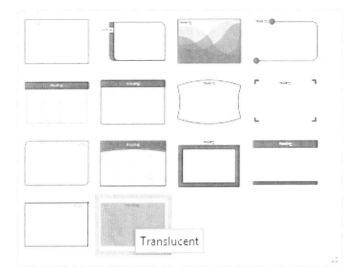

d) Select **Heading Style** from the ribbon.

e) Select the last heading style on the right, **Heading Style 4**.

f) Select the header and type *Draft Version*

2. Center the title text and increase the font to 24 pt.

a) Select the text of the diagram title so that it is highlighted in gray.

b) From **Home→Paragraph**, select the **Centered** text button.

c) In the **Font** group, select **24 pt**.

3. Save and close the file.

You may want to show LearnTO **Think Outside the Flowchart in Visio** from the CHOICE Course screen or have students navigate out to the Course screen and watch it themselves as a supplement to your instruction. If not, please remind students to visit the LearnTOs for this course on their CHOICE Course screen after class for supplemental information and additional resources.

> **Note:** For more information, check out the LearnTO **Think Outside the Flowchart in Visio** presentation from the **LearnTO** tile on the CHOICE Course screen.

Summary

In this lesson, you applied Visio's design features and inserted a container to improve the appearance of a diagram. You can use the properties of the shapes and connectors to enhance their appearance. The themes and variants that provide distinctive color schemes and shapes help you to give your Visio drawing a professional look, without affecting the aesthetic concept of the theme. Containers allow you to visually group shapes in complex drawings to ensure that your work is better organized and clearer.

Which design feature would be most helpful to you in your work?

A: Answers will vary, but may include the variety themes and variants, or the connector arrow shape options.

Does your organization have a theme that is used in their documents? How is it similar or different from Visio's built-in themes?

A: Answers will vary, but may include more traditional or modern themes.

Note: Check your CHOICE Course screen for opportunities to interact with your classmates, peers, and the larger CHOICE online community about the topics covered in this course or other topics you are interested in. From the Course screen you can also access available resources for a more continuous learning experience.

Encourage students to use the social networking tools provided on the CHOICE Course screen to follow up with their peers after the course is completed for further discussion and resources to support continued learning.

Course Follow-Up

In this course, you learned the basics of Visio and created a workflow diagram, an organizational chart, a cross-function flowchart, and a network diagram. In addition, you used Visio's design features to make a more professional-looking product.

What's Next?

Now that you have learned the fundamentals of Visio 2016 and have gained the skills to make a variety of diagrams, you can continue to *Microsoft® Visio® 2016: Part 2,* where you will create and enhance charts and diagrams by using the advanced features of Visio 2016. Or you can take any of the other courses that cover the products in Microsoft's suite of Office courses.

You are encouraged to explore Visio further by actively participating in any of the social media forums set up by your instructor or training administrator through the **Social Media** tile on the CHOICE Course screen.

A | New Features in Visio 2016

Visio 2016 has a number of new features and a set of features that have been enhanced compared to the previous Visio version, Visio 2013. These features are briefly described in the table.

Feature Name	Feature Type	Allows You To
Quick Import	New	Import data from Excel into Visio in fewer steps compared to the Import Wizard.
Information Rights Management Protection	New	Protect sensitive information by defining the users who can access the file and indicate whether the user can edit or only view the file.
Starter Diagrams	New	Use built-in layouts for creating some types of diagrams instead of having to start with the blank template for all your diagrams.
Tell Me	New	Locate and perform specific action or command without having to navigate the interface for locating the command.
Office Themes	New	Use the three new Office themes for your Visio interface elements.
Office Layout Shapes	Enhancement	Use modern shapes in your office layout diagrams.
Site Plan Shapes	Enhancement	View detailed design of site plan while providing additional shapes.
Floor Plan Shapes	Enhancement	View detailed design of your floor plan by providing redesigned shapes.
Home Plan Shapes	Enhancement	Utilize modern shapes in your home plan.
Electrical Diagram Shapes	Enhancement	Use updated shapes that are compatible with IEEE standard and provide more details related to your diagrams.

 Note: For complete details of each of the new features in Visio 2016, refer to the URL **https://support.office.com/en-us/article/What-s-new-in-Visio-2016-798f4f39-2833-486b-9ae9-55162672102e**.

Mastery Builders

Mastery Builders are provided for certain lessons as additional learning resources for this course. Mastery Builders are developed for selected lessons within a course in cases when they seem most instructionally useful as well as technically feasible. In general, Mastery Builders are supplemental, optional unguided practice and may or may not be performed as part of the classroom activities. Your instructor will consider setup requirements, classroom timing, and instructional needs to determine which Mastery Builders are appropriate for you to perform, and at what point during the class. If you do not perform the Mastery Builders in class, your instructor can tell you if you can perform them independently as self-study, and if there are any special setup requirements.

Mastery Builder 2–1
Adding More Departments to the IVR Diagram

Activity Time: 15 minutes

Data File
C:\091071Data\Working with Workflow Diagram Tools\IVR Lab.vsdx

Scenario
Add more departments to the IVR diagram, as shown in the following diagram.

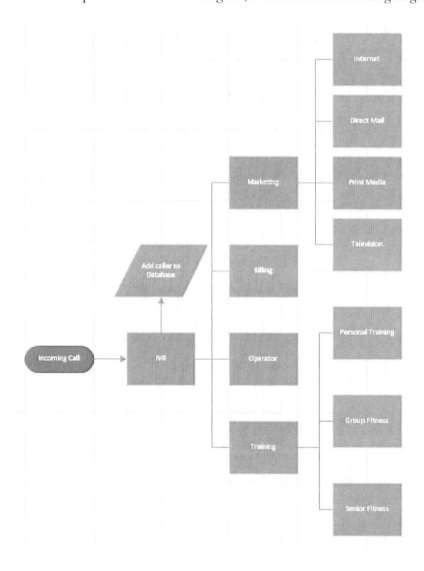

1. Add another department, **Marketing,** and place it above **Billing**.

2. Use the multi-tree square connector from the **Connectors** stencil. Drag the yellow handle in the middle of the connector's main branch to make more connections.

 Note: For viewing the handles of the multi-tree square connector clearly, increase the Zoom percentage of the drawing to 200% or above.

3. Add four sub-departments to **Marketing**: **Internet**, **Direct Mail**, **Print Media**, and **Television**. Add connections as needed.

4. Add three more sub-departments to **Training**: **Personal Training**, **Group Fitness**, and **Senior Fitness**.

5. Save the file as *My IVR Lab.vsdx* and close the file.

Mastery Builder 3–1
Creating an Organization Chart with Additional Fields

Activity Time: 15 minutes

Scenario

B&B Fitness is under negotiations with Premier Fashion House to create a custom fitness program. The creative team asked you to create an organization chart of Premier Fashion House to use in their presentation. They have supplied you with a table with the following information that they would like on the chart.

Name	Reports To	Title	Department	Telephone Ext.
Hugo Boss		CEO	Executive	1000
Tommy Hilfiger	Hugo Boss	VP	Product Dev.	8881
Liz Claiborne	Hugo Boss	VP	Legacy	8882
Louis Vuitton	Hugo Boss	VP	Accessories	8883
Christian Louboutin	Liz Claiborne	Designer	Legacy	8884
Christian Dior	Tommy Hilfiger	Designer	Product Dev.	8885
Roberto Cavalli	Tommy Hilfiger	Designer	Product Dev.	8886
Ploni Almoni	Tommy Hilfiger	Tailor	Product Dev.	8887

1. Create an organizational chart either manually or by using the wizard.

2. Use the **Coin** shape style.

3. Create additional fields so that the telephone and title are displayed in block 1 and the name in block 2.
   a) On the **Org Chart** tab, Shapes group, select the dialog box launcher to open the **Options** dialog box.
   b) Select the **Fields** tab.
   c) For the upper block, block 1 of the shape, check **Telephone Ext**.

4. Save the file as *My Premier Org Chart.vsdx* and close the file.

Mastery Builder 4–1
Creating a B&B Fitness Floor Plan

Activity Time: 15 minutes

Scenario
Create the following floor plan for B&B Fitness' flagship fitness center.

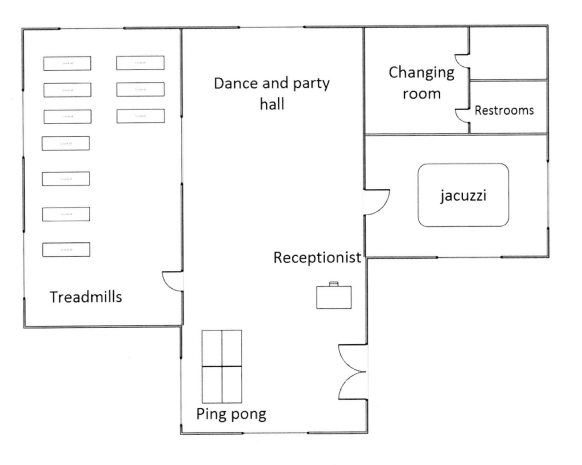

1. Include the room shapes to create the required number of rooms and label the rooms as given in the layout.

2. Reposition the rooms to match the layout.

3. Add basic shapes and door shapes at the locations indicated in the layout.

4. After creating the floor plan, save the file as *My B&B Fitness Floor Plan.vsdx* and close the file.

Mastery Builder 5–1

Revising the Sales Process Cross-Functional Flow Chart

Activity Time: 15 minutes

Data File

C:\091071Data\Building a Cross-Functional Flowchart\B&B Fitness Sales Process Lab.vsdx

Scenario

Due to budget restrictions, a consultant will no longer be a part of the sales process. Change the sales process cross-functional flowchart so that there is no longer a consultant band, and the sales department now decides if a non-standard product can be created and defines it. Sales also creates and presents the Shared Understanding PowerPoint presentation.

Because the drawing is now smaller, change the orientation from horizontal to vertical, and then readjust the positions of the shapes and connectors to make a more aesthetic result.

---

1. Open the file **B&B Fitness Sales Process Lab.vsdx** and move the flowchart shapes from the **Consultant** band to the **Sales Mgt** band.

2. Remove the **Consultant** band.

3. Move the **Present Shared Understanding Powerpt** box from the **Acct. Rep** band to the **Sales Mgt** band.

4. Realign the shapes and connectors as required.

5. After creating the diagram, save the file as *My B&B Fitness Sales Process Lab.vsdx* and close the file.

Mastery Builder 6-1
Creating a Radial Network

Activity Time: 15 minutes

Scenario

Use the Basic Network 3-D template from the Network template category to create the radial network shown here.

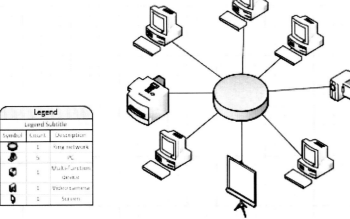

---

1. Drag the **Ring Network** shape and position it at the center of the diagram.

2. Drag and position the PCs around the ring in the arrangement indicated in the diagram. **Hint:** Connect the arrows extending from the ring to the PCs by using the glue-to-connection-point option.

3. Drag and connect the **Multi-function device**, **Video camera**, and the **Screen** as given in the diagram.

4. Add the **Legend** to the diagram.

5. After creating the diagram, save the file as *My Radial Network.vsdx* and close the file.

Mastery Builder 7–1

Revising the Inventory Process Cross–Functional Flow Chart

Activity Time: 15 minutes

Data File

C:\091071Data\Styling a Diagram\Fitness Inventory with Draft.vsdx

Scenario

The management has decided not to create a draft version of the inventory report this year, but plans to do it next year. You decide to copy the draft version container onto page 2 of the diagram, remove the container from page 1 of the diagram, and connect the rest of the shapes together. The result should look like the following image.

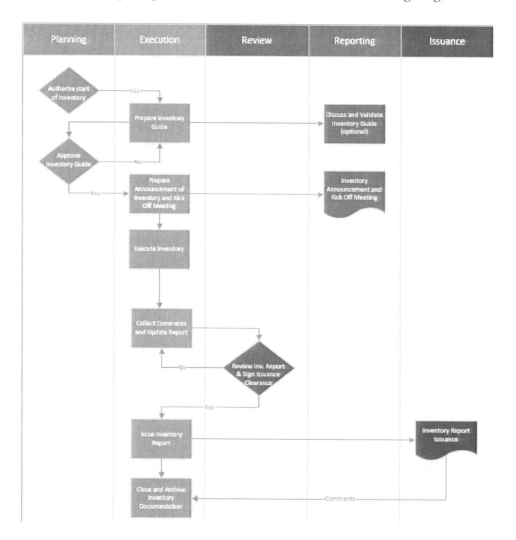

1. Create an additional page by selecting the + sign at the bottom of the page.

2. Copy the container to page 2 and delete it from page 1.

3. Make any necessary corrections to the diagram to connect the remaining shapes together.

4. Save the file as *My Fitness Inventory No Draft.vsdx* and close the file.

Glossary

connection points
Special types of points to which you can glue connectors and shapes. These points allow you to move the shapes around along with the glued connectors.

connectors
One-dimensional entities that connect shapes. They are attached to shapes either as a whole or to specific connection points on a shape.

containers
Refers to the special type of objects that allow you to organize and define logical groupings when working with complex drawings in Visio.

cross–functional flowchart
A special type of flowchart that is used to illustrate a process flow involving multiple departments, companies, functions, or tasks, or the division of labor in an integrated process.

Department Organization Chart
One of the built-in starter diagrams in the Organization Chart Wizard template in Visio 2016. It can show the hierarchy levels along with the reporting relationships.

dynamic grid
Provides alignment guides that appear as you drag a shape near an existing shape, or next to a page margin.

Favorites stencil
A stencil to which you can save shapes to easily access them in one place. The Favorites stencil is created automatically when you install Visio and is located in More Shapes under My Shapes. You can also store shapes you've found in searches here, as well as any shapes you've modified or created.

gluing
A property of connectors that allows them to remain connected to a shape, either with respect to the whole shape or to a specific connection point on a shape.

Hierarchical Organization Chart
A built-in starter diagram in the Organization Chart Wizard template in Visio 2016. It allows you to show your organization levels along with the reporting relationships.

layers
Refers to objects similar to clear drawing sheets that are placed on top of one another, merging to produce a finished drawing. Layers provide additional control over elements in a drawing.

lists
Special types of containers that are available only in some specific Visio templates to automatically sequence the items that are placed in them.

live preview

A dynamic feature that shows the result of an intended selection as the pointer hovers above it. This allows you to view choices before actually applying them.

master

A shape that is contained in a stencil. When the master is dragged to the drawing page, an instance of it is created there. The instance is linked to the master on the local stencil and inherits its behavior and appearance.

Microsoft Office 365

A collection of cloud-based Office applications (including Outlook, Word, PowerPoint, Excel, and OneNote), and services (including Lync, SharePoint, and Exchange) that provide tools for communication, mail, and document sharing. These applications and services are stored on Microsoft servers and accessed through the Internet with a web browser.

network diagram

A Visio diagram type that uses symbols to represent common network devices such as servers and routers, and the style of lines between them indicates the type of connection. These diagrams can be made at different scales to show various levels of granularity.

OneDrive

Microsoft's cloud-based file storage. Files on OneDrive are available on multiple PCs, smartphones, and even non-Windows devices when the OneDrive app is installed on them.

OPC

(Open Packaging Conventions) A container-file technology that combines XML and non-XML files into a single entity. OPC files can be opened by using a ZIP utility.

organization chart

Allows you to depict the systematic flow of authority and responsibility within an organization in your drawing.

Organization Chart Wizard

The tool provided by Visio for automating the creation of an organization chart.

pan

Shift the center point of the view to another part of the drawing without changing the magnification.

Quick Shapes

A feature that provides easy access to frequently used shapes as you draw without having to drag them from the stencil. The Quick Shapes area at the top of each stencil holds four to six of the most frequently used shapes. When Autoconnect is activated and you point at a shape in the drawing, the Quick Shapes appear in a mini toolbar and can be previewed and selected. The Quick Shapes are also included in the Favorites stencil.

Shape Data

A set of contextually relevant fields that are a built-in property of a shape.

shapes

Two-dimensional entities that are the building blocks of a Visio drawing. Shapes are contained in stencils.

snap

Snapping pulls shapes to ruler subdivisions, grid lines, guides, or guide points so that you do not have to place a shape in the exact position manually. There are advanced settings to control what types of objects shapes snap to and the snap strength (amount of attraction that an object exerts).

starter diagram

The built-in diagrams of Visio 2016, which provide suitable layouts according to the template category that help you to build your diagram easily.

stencil

A collection of related shapes that are used to create a specific type of diagram, such as a flowchart or road map.

swimlanes
Refers to vertical or horizontal bands that represent functional units, such as departments, teams, or even individuals in cross-functional flowcharts.

Tell Me
A new feature in Visio 2016 that enables you to quickly find specific functions or commands within the Visio interface.

template
A kit that contains the menus, toolbars, stencils, and shapes that you need to create a specific type of drawing, such as an organization chart or a timeline.

Text dialog box
Allows you to apply additional formatting options, such as transparency, spacing, margins, and background color that are not available by default on the ribbon.

theme
A predefined set of colors and styles that you can quickly apply to a drawing.

Visio
A diagramming application that contains tools for creating professional-looking drawings to represent data, systems, and processes.

VSD
The Visio 2003 – 2010 drawing file format.

VSDX
The Visio 2013 or above drawing file format, based upon Open Packaging Conventions and XML.

XML
(Extensible Markup Language) A markup language for encoding documents. XML can be read by humans and machines.

zoom
Feature that increases or decreases the magnification.

Index

091071I rev 1.0
ISBN-13 978-1-4246-2628-1
ISBN-10 1-4246-2628-5